The history of

The Guild Inn

Carole M. Lidgold

2000 Toronto, Ontario

Published by
Brookridge Publishing House
Scarborough, Ontario

Canadian Cataloguing in Publication Data

Lidgold, Carole M.
The History of the Guild Inn

Includes bibliographical references and index
ISBN # 0-9698244-8-3

1. Guild of All Arts—History.
2. Arts and crafts movement—Ontario—Toronto—History
3. Guild Inn (Toronto, Ont.)—History. I. Title

NK842.T6L52 2000 745'.09713'541 C00-930080-5

Cover design and textual layout by Karen Petherick

Edited by Abbeyfield Company

Sketches by Atenn Chong
Hugh Walker

Indexed by: Jack Coughlin, Lochleven Publishers

Printed and bound in Canada by Webcom Limited

Dedicated to

the memory of

Rosa and Spencer Clark

Contents

The Author beside her favourite sculpture

Foreword

I remember the times my father drove mother, my sister Shirley and I down a terrifying road to visit the Guild Inn. Now I drive up and down Guildwood Parkway without fear. I'd heard of craftsmen at the Guild Inn but never knew anything about them. They were gone by the time my family and I moved into Guildwood Village fourteen years ago. I've always been curious about the Guild Inn's past. Then at a meeting on the future of the Inn, in conversation with Dorsey James in September 1998, I realized that no history had been written. I was suddenly excited and decided to plunge into the files and write the history myself.

The research has finally answered my many questions and surprised me with its story. This is the story, in brief, as not everything could be included. The Breithaupt Hewetson Clark Collection files, at the University of Waterloo library, contain almost the entire history as Rosa and Spencer Clark apparently never threw anything away in over 50 years. The Toronto Archives contain files and more files in the Guild office.

I also wanted to, and did, include stories of the artisans and craftspeople who were an integral part of the Guild of All Arts. Some are deceased, others I couldn't interview.

Spencer Clark wrote the history of the Guild Inn for the celebration of its 50 years. However, due to costs, it was never published. The manuscript is part of the collection at Waterloo University.

In the year 2000, when historians are reviewing the past century, I offer this book as my contribution. The Guild Inn was an arts community experiment that lasted until Spencer Clark's death in 1986, and leaves a lasting legacy of architecture from Toronto's past.

Carole M. Lidgold

Ranelagh Park

Colonel Harold Child Bickford
Sketch by Atenn Chong

Ranelagh Park

In 1914, atop the clay cliffs of Scarborough Bluffs, a two-storey chateau was built at Ranelagh Park, a summer home for Colonel Harold Child Bickford and his family.

The pseudo-Georgian chateau had servants' quarters on the second floor in the west wing above the kitchen. A school room was located here for Colonel. Bickford's seven children. In the east wing was a nursery for the youngest children as well as three bedrooms and a bathroom. The centre section contained four more bedrooms and a wide staircase. The staircase was, and still is, a grand stairway to the upper floor. Two bedrooms had access to the balcony that stretched across the centre portion of the chateau, overlooking Lake Ontario.

Below the balcony, on the main level is a large verandah. Two doors, one from the living room and another from the dining room, lead onto the verandah. A hallway and the lower portion of the staircase are at the front of the chateau with the main entrance next to a library. The main floor of the western wing contained a large kitchen, a pantry and another room for the servants. Leading down from the servants quarters on the second floor, is a stairway into the kitchen. From the kitchen, a short hallway with stairs leads to an outside entrance. On the main floor of the eastern wing are three bedroom for guests with their own entrance. One bathroom and a two-piece washroom behind the staircase was used by the guests. One guest-room had a fireplace and on the other side of the wall, in the livingroom, is another fireplace.

A double-sided fireplace warmed the hallway and the library. On the second floor there was also a fireplace in the nursery and in an adjacent bedroom in the centre section. On the north side of the second floor, above the library, another bedroom also had a fireplace.

Under the centre portion of the chateau a basement contained a boiler room, storage room, a room to store fruit and vegetables and of course a laundry room. A passageway led outside to the west side of the building.

The chateau was white with many windows of varying sizes. The verandah was closed in with large arch-shaped windows and a door to the patio. A low stone wall, with a wide cement top, edged the patio.

The building known today as The Studio, was once part of a collection of buildings. One was a stable for ponies, as Harold Bickford was a polo player, the upper level used as a hayloft. There was a two-car garage with an apartment on the second level.

Harold Child Bickford
1876–1956

In 1876 in the city of Toronto at a house called Gore Vale, Harold Child Bickford was born. He was the last of four children born to Edward O. Bickford and his second wife, Emily. Harold had two brothers, Edward and Charles, and a sister Beatrice. Harold was educated at Trinity College School in the town of Port Hope, Ontario. In 1895, at the age of 19, he joined the military. One of the least-known military men, possibly because newspaper reporters could not get an interview. He never demanded anyone do what he himself would not do. A Brigadier-General, he retired in 1919.

His military career began with the Govenor General's Body Guards. Two years later, 1897, Harold was posted to England and joined the 6th Dragoon Guards (Carabiniers) and served as an officer with the British Army in India, then in the South African War. Recommended by Sir Douglas Haig, Commander-in-Chief of the British forces in France, Harold attended the military college in England, the only officer to take the course that year.

In 1901 in South Africa he became a hero. While loaded with ammunition, a bandolier belt over his shoulder, Private Hamilton of the Scots Greys rode his horse across the Assegai River. Swept off his horse he began to sink. Captain Bickford jumped in, saved him but the rushing water carried them both downstream, a quarter of a mile. The horse was never seen again and Captain Bickford received the Royal Humane Society's Bronze medal.

Earlier in his career in South Africa, Harold was part of the operations in the Orange Free State. He was also at Paardeburg in the actions at Poplar Grove, Driefontein and Karee Siding. In May 1900 his regiment was in the Transvaal and saw action at Diamond Hill. From July, until November, he was part of the operation east of Pretoria with action at Reit Vell and Belfast. In September and October 1901 he was on the Zulu frontier of Natal. His regiment served in the Transvaal until 1902 and then moved to the Orange River Colony for two months.

When World War I began in 1914, Harold offered his services to the Canadian Expeditionary Forces in Valcartier, Quebec as Colonel Bickford. Appointed a General Staff Officer of Military District No. 2 in Ontario, he was responsible for training 100,000 troops recruited in Toronto. He did much to improve the welfare of the troops and helped organize the Military Athlete Association. However, he did not get to see action in France until 1918.

General Bickford was sent to Siberia in command of two Canadian battalions, the 259th and 260th, and in command of two British battalions that were never located by the Canadians. Unfortunately these battlions were involved in only one action, a rather humourous one.

The town of Skotova was attacked by the Bolsheviks. The allied forces at Vladivostok were ordered to make a counter attack—however only as a demonstration. The troops were excited at relieving the boredom of their lives in camp. A force was mustered that included two battalions of Japanese, one company of Canadians, and eight officers. French troops included 84 soldiers and five officers. The Italian contingent consisted of 20 soldiers and one officer. Also involved were 15 Czecho-Slovaks with one officer, plus six Chinese and one officer.

General Bickford was not allowed to go with these troops as he out ranked the Japanese Colonel. The Canadian company was under the command of Major Mel Hart. General Bickford inspected the Canadian detachment and said, "The eyes of the world are on you."

The combined force took the train to Skotova and discovered that the Bolsheviks had already departed. There was one casulty. Back in camp the cooks were experimenting with a Japanese drink known as 'saki'. While accidently playing with a revolver, the French cook was shot. There was no glory, or story, to share with the world. General Bickford remained in Siberia until 1919.

Harold received eleven citations and was made a Companion of the Order of St. Michael and St. George. He received the Queen's medal with five clasps and the King's medal with two. France conferred on him the Croix de Guerre, while the Japanese gave him the Order of the Sacred Treasure.

When Harold retired he became a real estate broker. He used his chateau at Ranelagh Park, with its large quantity of property, to demonstrate that he was a bona fide realtor. However, the great depression relieved him of his wealth and he was forced to sell Ranelagh Park which was bought by the China Mission Seminary. In 1921 he moved his family, his wife Mary Davidson Bickford, two sons and five daughters to Buffalo, New York. He was divorced from Mary and she died in 1935 of appendicitis.

In Buffalo, Harold regained his fortune through the real estate market and became a prominent member of society. A street, in the area where he built a housing development, was named after him as well as after his wife and several daughters. To commemorate the Bickford family, in Toronto, Bickford Park Collegiate and Bickford Park was named for them. To remember him as a previous owner of Ranelagh Park, now the Guild Inn, one of the conference rooms is named the Bickford Room.

During the 1940s Harold and his daugher visited the Guild Inn and met Spencer Clark. Another daughter, Millicent, visited the Inn in 1968.

During the later years of his life, Harold resided in Muskoka and Florida. He was a member in many sports-oriented clubs such as the Royal Yacht Club in Toronto, the Bath Club of London, England. In Buffalo, New York, he was a member of the Saturn Club, the Athletic Club and the Country Club.

At 79 years of age, on Feb. 18th, 1956, he died at the home of his daughter Mary in Spokane. Washington and is buried in St. James Cemetary, Toronto.

China Mission Seminary

China Mission Seminary
Photo from the collection of Richard Schofield

St. Francis Xavier China Mission Seminary 1921–1923

On October 18th, 1921, Ranelagh Park became the China Mission College. Father J. M. Fraser bought the property for $35,000. with three mortgages. The first mortgage of $7,500 at 6% was due in August 1924 to Mr. N. M. Gilchrist. The downpayment was $10,000.The second mortgage for $10,000 was from the estate of Sir John C. Eaton at 6% due February 1926. The third mortgage was held by Harold Bickford for $7,500 at 6% interest, due October 1926.

The China Mission was part of Father Fraser's dream to send trained missionaries to China. He was born in Bamphshire, Scotland on June 28, 1877, the ninth of eleven children. The family emigrated to Toronto where his father built a house on Bathurst Street.

In Italy in 1901, Father Fraser was ordained and the next year was in China as a missionary. He spent approximately ten years at Ning-po, south of Shanghai and realized that one man alone can't make a difference in a country of millions.

In the United States in 1911 he influenced Mary Knoll to start a China mission. As well he was influential in the founding of the Irish St. Columban Mission. Then he decided to organize his own mission college in Canada.

In Alimonte, Ontario, 35 miles from Ottawa, an old school became vacant, which had also served as a convent for the Sisters of St. Joseph. In 1918 Father Fraser received approval from Archbishop Gauthier of Ottawa to purchase the school and establish his mission college.

The college began with 12 students who studied Chinese, Latin, Philosophy and Theology. By 1920 the student population overflowed to a house next door and larger quarters were needed. In 1921 Archbishop McNeil of Toronto wrote to Father Fraser about a house for sale in Scarborough, a private home owned by General Bickford. However he noted that it was three-quarters of a mile from Kingston Rd., the highway, and driving at 10–12 miles an hour, took four minutes to get to the house.

Ranelagh Park was purchased and became a boarding school for missionaries training for work in China. Soon there were more students than could be accommodated and Father Fraser appealed for funds to build a larger mission college. In 1923, the China Mission College was sold to Mr. R.V. Look for $50,000. Although the building had been sold, the China Mission Seminary was allowed to remain until their new building (located at Brimley Rd. and Kingston Rd.) was completed in 1924.

Father Fraser engaged a new rector for the college, Dr. John E. McRae, and went back to China taking two missionaries with him. He returned to the mission at Ning-po where he remained until 1941.

After a General Council meeting in Canada, Father Fraser attempted to return to China. In Manila, the Philippines, he was interred as a prisoner of war and the mission society couldn't locate him for four years. After the war he returned to China until 1949 when he came to Canada for a General Chapter meeting.

Father Fraser was unable to return to China as it was under control of the communists. Instead he went to Japan. Father Fraser returned to Canada to raise funds for the building of the western wing of the Scarborough Foreign Mission Society but soon departed to Japan. On September 3rd, 1962 he died peacefully in his sleep at age 85.

Cliff Acres

Richard V. Look
Sketch by Atenn Chong

Cliff Acres
1923–1932

In 1923, a 6'8" business man from Kentucky purchased the China Mission College as a summer home. Richard Veech Look was born June 7, 1878 in Louisville, Kentucky and came to Canada in 1913. He was married to Margaretta, the daughter of Lieutenant Brooke of the U. S. Army, and they had two sons.

He was employed with the American Creosoting Company and became an assistant to the president, in Chicago, in 1908. In 1912 he was appointed vice-president then sent to Canada as president of the Canada Creosoting Co. Ltd. Later executive positions included president and director of the Vancouver Creosoting, Dominion Tar & Chemical, Alberta Wood Preserving and Alexander Murray & Co., Montreal.

In 1927 the head offices for these companies were moved to Montreal, Quebec. Richard Look and his family also moved there. From 1927 until 1932 Cliff Acres remained empty, maintained by a caretaker. In 1932 this property was purchased by Rosa Breithaupt Hewetson, who a few months later married Spencer Clark.

Rosa Melvina Breithaupt
Photo from the collection of The Guild

Rosa Breithaupt Hewetson

Rosa Breithaupt Hewetson
1888–1981

On June 19, 1888, Rosa Melvina Breithaupt was born to a prominent family in Berlin, Ontario. During WWI the town's name was changed to Kitchener after well-known Lord Kitchener of World War I. Her family, of German heritage belonging to the Lutheran Church, believed in public service with social concerns and also supported the arts. Rosa's father, Louis J. Breithaupt, worked in a leather company started by his father. Her mother was Emma Devitt. She was one of eight children, five girls and three boys, and one of her brothers, Louis O. Breithaupt, become the Lieutenant-Governor of Ontario. Rosa herself, although she refrained from seeking the limelight, would leave a lasting legacy in following her family's devotion to improving social conditions.

A shy child, Rosa was talented in music and art. She enjoyed a happy childhood involved in her church and family. As a choir member she was also a soloist. A diary entry on January 19, 1916 records that she sang "Softly and Tenderly" at a church meeting. Her family owned a large houseboat docked on Georgian Bay that slept 25 people. It had to be caulked each year to prevent leaks. Finally the family purchased property on an island and towed the houseboat there. This property is still owned and used by Breithaupt descendants.

Educated in Whitby at the Ontario Ladies College, Rosa majored in art and graduated in 1909 as a gold medallist. She was an accomplished pianist and could have had a musical career in this field. Instead she became involved in the Christian Endeavour Movement where she met her first husband, Russell Hewetson, whose company made shoes. Her diaries record the times he visited her family on weekends and when he left, but she never wrote out her feelings for him. The diaries record the events of her life but not her emotions. In 1917 Rosa married Russell at her home under a canopy erected in the drawing room, by Rev. J.P. Hauch, pastor of Zion Evangelical Church. A poem, the author unknown, tells of their marriage. She was 29 years old when she married.

A Shoe and Leather Romance

Listen folks, we've a word to say,
See that couple—yep! Married to-day
With happy smiles and that big grip,
Easy to see it's their wedding trip.

They surely think they are in clover,
Guess they think they put one over,
But they'll find out before they're through,
That we have put one over too.

But take it from us, they're a real fine pair
The kind you don't meet everywhere.
Kid 'em a bit—they won't get sore,
You see they were never married before.

What's that you said? What's his name,
His first is Russell—he's gathered fame
Making shoes for the little tot,
Perhaps the kind you've often bot!

He always works to make others glad,
The kind of guy that's never sad.
That big round face with it's happy smile
He carries with him all the while.

And the lady? Who is she?
His better half as you can see.
Call her Rosa—she won't mind,
She's also one of the jolly kind.

How does it happen they're joined together?
Russell makes shoes—her dad makes leather.
"Spose they happened to meet by chance,
A regular Shoe and Leather Romance.

Now if you knew them as well as we
You'd hope they'll always happy be.
So altogether—Let her rip
Show the pair a real live trip.

Rosa called their home in Brampton, Ontario "The Castle". They had four children, three daughters, Ruth, Rosemary, Dorothy and a son, Russell. Their first anniversary they were both ill, possibly from a bad cold, as Rosa's diary records the numerous times she suffered this affliction. In 1928, eleven years after they were married, Russell became ill with pneumonia and suddenly died, leaving Rosa with four young children and a shoe company to run.

Love and Life[1]
It is the Christmas tonight
That love and life are forever more
Gifts which our King has brought
Out of His Royal store.

Gifts which he bids us take
And cherish through our days of joy and pain
And rise for his dear sake
And bring to Him again.

And lay before His feet
For though our love is weak
Our faith is dim
His love can make complete
Gifts which we use for Him.

1 *Written in the back of a diary from 1928.*

Written by Rosa on a scrap of loose paper, a year after the death of Russell, dated October 5, 1929, is the following prayer:

> Dear Jesus and heavenly Father. We want to do thy will on earth. We want to measure up to the highest thoughts thou hast for us. Give us power from on high—the power of the Holy Spirit so richly promised to if we only accept. Life here is so short, help us to do and dare for Thee, while it is yet day—that we may be worthy of a place with our loved ones who have gone before and who are even now nearer than we can humanly comprehend. Help us to live more and more in the spirit forgetting the things of the flesh. Thou knowest our inmost thoughts, dear Saviour, better than we can frame them. Help us always to forget self in the broader union of helping others. For Jesus sake. Amen.

Rosa did very well managing her husband's company but she wanted to make changes. Her idea was to make the company a co-operative venture with the employees on a profit-sharing basis. During Rosa's and Russell's wedding trip to the United States they had learned of a man named Arthur Nash who inspired them to this business concept. He had been a businessman and after his retirement he had received a registered letter about the demise of the textile mill of which he had been a shareholder. This mill was a sweatshop where elderly women worked as needle workers for $4.00 a week. There were children who should have been in school. At this time there was no social legislation regulating working conditions, no child labour laws, no minimum wage laws, no workman's compensation, no pension schemes and no unemployment insurance.

Arthur Nash had been appalled at the working conditions and ashamed that his income was derived from workers in such a sad state of employment. He persuaded the creditors to let him take over the company, then talked to the employees about his plans. He stated that he would put his money back into the business and immediately increase wages. If the employees would trust him he would organize a profit-sharing programme. Seven years later the business was once again a profitable venture.

Rosa and Russell discussed plans to initiate a profit-sharing programme into the Hewetson Shoe Company. However, as Russell was not the main shareholder, nothing could be done until he could obtain these shares after his father's death. Unfortunately, Russell died before this could occur.

With help from H. Hapgood of the Columbia Conserve Co., who was also interested in promoting this style of ownership, Rosa tried to make this concept a workable plan. However, this idea did not evolve into anything that could be effective. She could not convince the other shareholders, Russell's family, that her plan would be good for the employees as well as for the shareholders.

In a file at the Doris Lewis Rare Books Room at Waterloo University, titled "Rosa's Vision", is a draft of a letter to her in-laws. The following is an excerpt of her thoughts.

> "...Father repeatedly told me not to worry as far as financial matters were concerned for Russell's family would share 1/5 just as if R. were here.
> "...Father gave me to understand those shares would still revert to his estate for he said the girls all signed papers. However as far as I can see only one paper signed.
> "...now four sons-in-law who did practically nothing before R. going, together have half the say and they are already speaking with a good deal of authority.
> "...I am never going to be ignorant about things again if possible. The fact that I am now sole executrix of R's estate has been impressed upon me and I have every right to know what is going on in the business for that is where our living will come from.
> "...R's vision was years ahead of his time. He could see the necessity of a greater brotherhood on earth, so as to carry out the Bible teachings—and that was all because the Spirit of God was working through him when he left ministry to help support family.

"...As you know, it was last fall these ideas gripped me more forcibly than ever and I felt the spiritual urge to do something for others and naturally when it was Russell's spirit guiding, it seemed to direct along lines we had partly planned when he was here in the flesh...

"...giving gifts is not so much the idea now as giving opportunities. A man does not want to be indebted to you for a gift but will thank you for an opportunity to help develop things himself. *(Filene)*

"...I have gone through the greatest sorrow so really feel I have a spiritual contribution to make as also some business knowledge through Russell talking everything over with me. Also helped him in various ways with ideas, styles, etc.

"...Mother, let us as a family get together...get expert advice and do something to make the town, the province, the Dominion, yea even the world take notice...

"I am more anxious to leave the principals of the golden rule with my children than I am to amass more money for them.

"...I am very much of the idea Mother, that if something bigger and better cannot be done, my lot will eventually be cast in other circles where I can expound and work out the visions of a bigger brotherhood I clearly see...

"...If I can help work out something in life to help others more, I have a feeling that my grief and loneliness will be diminished...

Draft letter dated March 1, 1932

"...I can't sit back any longer. I can see the trend of the world activities...are we going to act or are we going to sit by with dumbness...I see a great opportunity for being the pioneers practically in a new industrial era in Canada. We can be the first Producers Co-operative on a big scale..."

Rosa began working with Henri Lassere of the University of Toronto. She was one of the founders of the Robert Owen Foundation, an organization to promote ideas of social concerns. Also involved in this foundation was H. Spencer Clark. An entry in Rosa's diary gives this statement: "Remember Lot's wife"[2].

Rosa was a beautiful woman with blue eyes and she loved to be well-dressed. She loved traveling and her favourite perfume (mentioned by one of her caregivers in her later years) was Chanel No. 5. She was an excellent organizer with a good business sense. She had her ideals, dreams, and knew how to do what she wanted. She also had the money to use in fulfilling these dreams.

In 1932, at the age of 44, a widow for four years with four small children, she began a new venture and purchased a property in Scarborough known as Cliff Acres. Excited, she discussed her new project with a friend and invited him for a visit. She changed the direction of her life, as well as that of her friend H. Spencer Clark.

---

2 *A story from the Bible.*

Letters to Rosa

Letters to Rosa

Spencer Clark had a decision to make that would transform his entire life and fulfill a fantasy he thought would never happen. In this letter written to Mrs. Rosa Hewetson in 1932 he poured out his feelings knowing she would understand but unsure of the answer he would receive. The following are excepts from his 27 page letter.

"This letter will be a little different, I'm afraid, than any that have preceded it. I have been troubled of late and I need very much the advice of a woman who understands—one who understands not only men and women and life's relationships, but as well the purposes which motivates some of our lives."

"A decade ago after meeting and talking with Arthur Nash, I placed my life on the altar of a definite work to be done—the importance of which I felt then, and increasingly since, ranked as high if not higher than any other of which I know. That has been as it were, my first love always; and my personal life and satisfaction have generally come second—not that the latter have not frequently, indeed almost incessantly, fought for first place. I have long wanted to be married and have foreseen some day when that would come with all its fullness. But the handicaps have been great and the field of choice strictly limited. I have first and foremost demanded a person possessed of a vision similar to my own—not that I wanted her to sacrifice anything to mine, but that she should have, independently and fervently, developed it; so that we might completely unite, devoted to some greater object outside ourselves; and enjoy as a by-product, as I have also always felt, would be the case, a greater, richer, fuller communion together."

"...We are standing on the threshold of great changes—as great or greater than any that have gone before—conscious evolution can direct them aright—unconscious undirected evolution is dangerous and frequently results in retrogression as past civilizations have amply witnessed. Then too, in the companion, full-partner that I have envisioned, I wanted the capacities to put such visions into practice, at least to sow the seeds, and we should hope to nurture them to ripe fruition—that has meant education at least comparable or surpassing my own, (though possibly self-acquired). It has meant more than education and ideals; it has meant experience as well, one who knows the hard world of realities and one who can keep a faith despite the experiences which might and do turn others to cynics. It has meant a balance between visions and practice for such experiments in our day must perforce be as scientific as ideal. And then again last, but far from least, my own emotional and psychical self have wanted all the lovely, womanly qualities—altogether one whom I could not only admire, respect and work with in complete unison and harmony, but wholly emotionally psychically and physically love with my whole soul and being."

"Perhaps it is no wonder I am not married—and yet a certain faith has always lingered that such a one would sooner or later come upon the horizon of my activity; or rather that we should both arrive upon the same scene, bent upon the same cause, together. For years I thought I knew of such a one, and the fantasy hovered over me. I approached this state with others; but instincts cautioned in time as some elements were missing, or as the fantasy of the one shone with brighter light. Then finally the opportunity came with the one of the fantasy—amid all the well-conditioned surroundings of one of the romantic beauty spots of old Europe—but—I found my fantasy afar from the one around whom it had been built. Almost all was perfection lovelier, more beautiful, more capable than ever—but—more conservative—the drive, the passion for the greater goal had quieted. Duty called; I tore away—co-operatives, conferences, like-minded people and places, ammunition for the future fray. In recent months I have gone through fire and brimstone. Naturally of a somewhat high-strung nervous temperament the strain of over-effort, carrying several full-time jobs together, with numerous side interests—(I have felt worthwhile) activities, lending stimulation to others, a voluminous correspondence and various speeches—the sum total has reacted on a fully, if not more than normal sexual nature. Sublimation has not satisfied; indeed the nature of the work itself—in the realm of ideas and ideals has but seemed to stimulate the more to sexual nature and its demands. And I think that God meant that it should be so—that should come as the great and satisfying culmination of all that is beauty and good—crowning—glory of all creation! that that sacramental moment should embrace the seeds of life—new life born of love."

"But to return. Repression has accentuated nervous tension and the net result has been instability, inefficiency, semi-exhaustion, and often deep depression; but worst of all the fear that in endeavoring to put what, I have thought, my greater ends first, and denying the natural functions of life, I should in the very process, defeat the ends I have long held most dear."

"In mere distraction I turned to the one who had come second only to my old fantasy. We talked plans and there were most alluring possibilities ahead—we almost took the plunge. She has almost all the qualities I have wanted, and she does want to help; we have much affinity of spirit and I have great feeling for her—but three hours ago we reluctantly parted—for I had a confession to make—that demanded all the courage and honesty I could summon to make it then—in a moment that could have been all loveliness—that at last I felt The One had come—that I had talked with and known and felt the quivering pulse that emanated her—and I felt it in tune with my own. Mrs. Hewetson, it was you."

"Perhaps this is all just silly. Even so, there seemed then only one thing to do—be honest and frank in the extreme—and Mrs. Hewetson, I have felt you are one with whom one could be safely such. For long, I have admired you tremendously but other thoughts have been just not there. Lately they were put there by another and I immediately brushed them aside as absurd, and a little irritated that anyone should suggest that I even think such impertinence. But last week, when I first talked over the telephone with you about your new venture—and suddenly felt the girl in you burst forth and escape its prison bounds of the last few years—I saw you entirely anew. You were young again, as young as you are—and not the generation ahead of me as I had previously thought of you. Then when I talked with you later and felt the change that had come over you and saw you smile, the first time I think, I had ever—and really knew more of your long struggles and the influences that had played upon you as upon me—I was stirred—deeply stirred Mrs. Hewetson, I want to think with you, plan with you, feel with you, live with you, work with you, strive with you—that together we might bring something worthier, finer more beautiful to pass on this old world of ours."

"There do seem to be bonds of understanding in the air we breathe, and ought but similar basic, life attitudes and similar trains of thought could have directed our courses independently in so nearly parallel channels. Ought but such things and similar purposes in life could have independently attracted us both to such people as Arthur Nash, William Hapgood....others you discovered. Your readiness to give so much for your ideal has stirred me—your home, your means, yourself. I have had less to give but have already given practically all, and hope I shall always want to continue. But you are right—it is not sacrifice; it is life!

There has been an element of coincidence, and I hope it may prove one of God's wonder ones, that the real you should have emerged as I was approaching the end of my letter. Mrs. Hewetson, I want and need you—more—the work we are about needs us both. So at least mine does you.

If the years matter not to you, neither do they to me. I am 29. You can figure and divulge or not as you wish. It matters little; it is the attitude, the spirit, the vision, the hope, the affinity in these, that love that embraces them all that counts.

Mrs. Hewetson, I realize there is every likelihood that you have thoroughly intended to never remarry. You have already enjoyed the heaven of a perfect relationship. You have your children, you have your ideals and you have your work ahead. One might readily say your life was full. If so, I'm sorry for all I have said. But again, it may be that knowing what such a full, satisfying relationship giving energy, harmony, and the greatest beauty of all to life can mean, may make you want it again but all the more. Perhaps I am vain and bold to suppose for an instant that I could ever bring such completeness to you. Forgive me, Mrs. Hewetson, if I am the hope of helping to complete something of what tragedy denied that you and your husband should have completed together, has helped to spur me to give voice to my feelings toward you.

I realize too, that there are many restraining elements that might deter you, now or indefinitely even if you should return any similar feelings; but again the determination you have already shown to carry out what is inner-most in you despite the winds that blow—has provided another ray of hope.

Mrs. Hewetson, perhaps this is all just perfectly absurd and ridiculous. If so, please just say so frankly and I promise you to say no more about it. I shall still admire and respect, and will still be ready to confer and work with you and help in whatever way I can in all your splendid endeavors; and if we are both frank and honest, I think we can do so—without embarrassment—and with the outside world little knowing or suspecting what these pages have tried to say. And if such be the case, I shall have to, before very long, turn in another direction, for I cannot go on a great while longer as I have of recent months. The work demands too much.

But if, perchance, it is not so absurd, I do not ask you to give me any hope or assurance let alone commit yourself in anyway—you have I know too much to consider—your own work, your family and your husband's, your children (I shall love them as my own) and just making sure yourself—but if you just say "wait" I shall do so gladly—I shall battle on alone— await your time and do all I can to help.

Ever sincerely yours,
H. Spencer Clark

June 24, 1932

My dear Mrs. Hewetson:

Thank you ever so much for your quick reply to my letter. It was good of you to let me know so soon that it had at least been received in the same spirit of honesty, frankness and sincerity in which it had been written—as I was sure it would—else I should scarcely have dared to write it.

Yes, I'll "turn up" on Monday evening the 27th—out at Scarborough and I appreciate your trustfulness and readiness to talk with me more than I can say.

Ever sincerely
Spencer Clark

Rosa dear:

Just a few words at the close of the day—a day serene and serious intertwined with joy and ecstasy—and thought mingling with work. Rosa darling, I can scarcely realize that you have trusted me so much already—nor that the day I have so long waited for, worked for and gone through much alone for—should have come so near at last. Rosa, this is not to assume that you have committed yourself entirely yet—for I want you to be sure, as sure as I am now—but all that has come so far has been so worthwhile in itself to begin, to really know you—to love you and to have and to know your love in return—and to know that behind and through it all, and to fortify and enrich all the future, we have the deepest purposes and interests in life in common and at heart.

...Rosa Dear—you can have my love, all of it—for all time—whenever you want to take it—and then its strength will know no bounds—the bounds will become all bonds—bonds without bounds! More—you have it now! And another experience tonight has told me so again with ever more strength and surety...

With all my love—for always—

Spencer

...Rosa Dearest,

Everything wells up inside all at once and I wish I could stay with you altogether and talk and talk with you by the hours— and know through your love how good the world can be. It is good—will help to make it better—for scarcely anything was ever so perfect that it could not be made a little better—for such is life and God's evolving plan...

Love you, love you...

Yours forever

Spen

Rosa Breithaupt Hewetson and Herbert Spencer Clark were married at the Guild Inn on Sunday, August 7th, 1932.

The Wedding Day of Rosa and Spencer
Photo from the collection of The Guild

Family gathered for the wedding
Photo from the collection of The Guild

August 1934—Handwritten note to Rosa

Just a little added note Rosa darling...of deeper affection than one wanted to dictate to a stenographer. My but I miss your steadying influence with me and know when you are away how impossible it would be for me to run this very long alone. We need each other very much...

Herbert Spencer Clark

Herbert Spencer Clark
Photo from the Breithaupt Hewetson Clark Collection
University of Waterloo

Herbert Spencer Clark
1903–1986

On October 10, 1903 in Toronto, Ontario, a son was born to John and Esther Clark. The boy, their fourth child was never very healthy. They named him Herbert Spencer. During the summer months to help improve their son's health, the family consisting of five children, lived on Ward's Island in a cottage that was part building, part tent. Esther doted on her sickly son Spencer, and over the years told him that "he was destined for both greatness and goodness" something which she herself had been denied.

Spencer's family were involved in social democracy and good works. His grandfather John, worked in England for Cadbury's, a confectionery firm which pioneered the concept of a garden village. When his son John went to Canada for a visit with his brother who was pioneering near Burke's Falls, he fell in love with a girl named Esther and stayed there.

After their marriage, John worked for Lipton's and Ridgeway's, the food products industry, giving his family a comfortable middle-class life. The family were compulsive writers and avid photographers, capturing on film their life on Ward's Island. All five children, including Spencer, were involved in working for the betterment of society.

Spencer's cousin, Edith Roach, was engaged to Frederick Banting for several years. He, in later years, was the co-founder of insulin. Frederick spent a lot of time with the Clark family and often stayed with them in their home in Toronto.

Spencer grew up with high ideals and after graduating in 1924 from the University of Toronto School of Applied Sciences, became an engineer. He worked for the Ontario Hydro Electric Power Commission, and Taylor Electric in London, Ontario. He was dissatisfied with his life and was interested in the idea of a co-operatively owned business. However, he did not have the money nor the time to invest in one.

As part of a study group, Spencer went to Europe during the summer of 1931. Part of the trip was to Russia to observe their economic and social conditions. He was away for almost four months experiencing the conditions of a struggle between the Communists and Hitlerites. The banks had closed and newspapers were filled with the momentous events taking place.

On his return to Canada Spencer was asked to share his observations and was a sought-after speaker. He also became involved in the Robert Owen foundation where he met Mrs. Hewetson a widow with four young children. They became friends and discovered they had mutual goals and social consciences. Then in 1932 Mrs. Hewetson purchased a property in Scarborough and invited him for a visit. It was a visit that made him realize he could not continue alone in his endeavours to make the world a better place to live.

The Guild of All Arts

Photo from collection of The Guild

THE GUILD OF ALL ARTS

Purpose:

The guild of all arts draws inspiration from the guilds of old; it recognizes the necessity of a constructive approach in all activities that life might be lived more fully; it will strive to be a centre from which, always, will emanate a cultural influence for truth and beauty through all the medium of creative art; and will endeavour to play its part in evolving a well-integrated society providing through co-operation and democracy, a great opportunity for the self expression of all its members.

Rosa Hewetson Clark and the Great Elm Tree
From the collection of The Guild

The Guild of All Arts

"It was a time of experiment and invention in the arts, science, education and religion....David Pogue"

The year 1932 was a financially-troubled time for Rosa and Spencer to open a new business. Rosa still managed the Hewetson shoe business and received a comfortable income. Spencer invested all his personal savings in their vision of a democratic crafts co-operative. This was during the Great Depression which began in 1929 with the stock market crash. Employment was hard to find for workers, especially in the crafts industry. In Quebec the depression was less apparent as their economy was still based on small industries. Other parts of Canada depended on large manufacturing industries, companies which had been forced to scale down their operations. In urban areas, approximately one million unemployed Canadians searched for work. In Saskatchewan, dependant on wheat production, drought and grasshoppers reduced the acreage yield to about eleven bushels instead of 18. With fewer shipments the railways were forced to lay off their workers. Rosa and Spencer provided work and lodging for some of the unemployed and their families at The Guild of All Arts.

As well as the spectacular view from the bluffs, one of the things that attracted Rosa to this site was that it was one of the areas on the shore of Lake Ontario still heavily wooded. There was a variety of trees in the unspoiled forest, elms, big ash trees, maple, beech, sycamore and a rare species, the Changrae Hickory. At one time a white elm stretched up 125' high.

Spencer asked the Davey Tree Expert Co. to study it as the top portion had been hit by lightning and broken off. The trunk of this tree was hollow and beginning to rot. The company reported that the white elm was approximately 230 years old. The diameter of the tree was 7' 8" wide and its height at that time was 75' high. In 1940 the elm tree was held together by guy wires. It was a shell with two stumpy branches. A doorway was worn into its side large enough for a person to walk through. An article in the Evening Telegram, Saturday, September 14, 1940 by Rose MacDonald, estimated the tree's age to be 575 years old. In later years only the stump remained to show its once proud location as a fire decimated it. A young boy had been playing Indian in the cavity of the tree and started a fire there. It was impossible to extinguish the fire because of its hollowness and age so the tree was destroyed.

Rosa and Spencer honeymooned in a community called Roycroft in the United States, a craftsman's co-operative, much like they wanted to open in Scarborough where craftsmen lived, worked and sold their products.

Roycroft's founder was Elbert Hubbard, a successful soap company executive who acquired a house. He had loaned a man $500.00 which the man couldn't repay and had to relinquish his house. The house was located in East Aurora, N.Y., thirty minutes south of Buffalo. In 1895 the town was decaying but had good property qualities. Under Elbert's influence it became a model town with an Inn, a chapel, a printing plant, a school and a book bindery, on 500 acres with 200 acres of woodland.

Roycroft mean "King's crafter", a man who makes things for the king and was based on the English crafts complex of William Morris. Elbert trained girls and boys to become printers, binders, stenographers, weavers and copper founders. They were also taught music and art. The boys and girls were housed at Roycroft. The products they made were sold at a profit to expand the work of Roycroft.

Visitors stayed at the Inn for $2.50 per day in an elegant building with paintings on the walls and fine furnishings in the dining room. The girls and boys were also the waitresses and waiters. A quote of Elbert's is that "...East Aurora appeals so widely because it brings art and letters into action as a team to aid in making a living." He also said that, "Life without industry is guilt—industry without art is brutality."

Visitors as well as seeing craftspeople at work had many leisure opportunities, woods to stroll through, camps to stay in, tennis, golfing, canoeing and dances in the grove. As well as purchasing the craft items, visitors could buy the many books and moral cards written by Elbert, telling the story of Roycroft and the people the rooms were named after.

One time in dealing with an artist who did not worry about the cost of producing an item, nor the time to complete it, the artist stated, "An artist knows nothing about time and expense...He creates. That is enough ..."

On May 7, 1915 the ship Lusitania was torpedoed by the Germans and sank. One of the passengers was Elbert Hubbard. After his death, his son Elbert continued the work of Roycroft. Today the Roycroft Inn still operates. It is located near Roycroft Campus that has 14 "architecturally-significant" buildings where 500 skilled craftsmen lived and had their shops. The rate, in US dollars, for a suite in the inn is now $165.00.

The Guild House became a residence for the first craftsmen and the Studio building later became their workshops where they also taught and displayed their output. Pioneers had built their own cabins, furniture and almost everything they needed. Rosa and Spencer were surprised that these skills had been lost in so short a time and wanted to reactivate them.

Rosa and Spencer were not the only ones with the idea for a co-operative business. Miss Jessie Barber of the Women's Union, University of Toronto, had a similar dream. She wanted to develop for university students, in a country site, activities based on community life. Like Spencer she had travelled extensively looking for a location. There were many other social activists with similar ideas, but it appears that only Rosa and Spencer actually initiated their dream.

In a letter that Spencer wrote to Mr. Kennedy Young on January 24, 1934 he explained their reasons for starting the Guild Inn. The following are some excerpts from this letter.

> "...Mrs. Clark and I, even before our marriage and commencement of the Guild, had been together for some years...We have both been firmly convinced for many years that great changes were needed in the social and economic world. There must for instance, come a more equitable distribution of income. There must be economic securities, and the necessities of life for all. There must also be greater opportunities for the full development of self-expression of every individual. After these things are to be attained and become permanent, they must not be dependant only on the paternalistic good will of a few

At the back
From the collection of The Guild

> who might still own and control the basic industries. The only safety lies in the extension of co-operative and democratic principals wherein the entire working force of every industry, office and factory staffs alike would have a greater voice and control in the operation of the business. That business should be operated for the benefit of all, those who were actively engaged in it rather than primarily for the benefit of the absentee shareholders who are interested in dividends only..."

As well as housing these people, Rosa and Spencer had to feed them. Seven acres of the forty they purchased were planted with vegetables. There was one acre planted with buckwheat, and asparagus beds. Three men worked this garden containing 1000 raspberry bushes and several hundred blackberry bushes. Chickens, that had been purchased from Spencer's Aunt Mary, provided eggs. Ducks were acquired and there was hope of obtaining Jersey cows.

In the 1920s this area had been bought by real estate developers for a summer resort colony. Cottages had been built on 50' wide lots by 160' deep and sold as recreational properties. However, built on hard clay soil, these purchasers had great difficulty locating well water. In later years these cottages were sold and became year-round properties. The cottages were covered with tarpaper and tin, insulated for cold weather with cardboard and sawdust. Instead of a summer resort these cottages became a slum area.

After Rosa and Spencer began their co-operative, they needed more housing for the craftsmen and their families. They began buying these slum cottages as housing for them as well as for their staff. Some cottages were too decrepitated and were torn down. The Guild was in an area isolated from transportation and it was not easy for staff to travel to work. To keep staff Rosa and Spencer were forced to offer room and board as well as a salary.

In 1932 a driver could not deliver an order from Aikenhead's Hardware store. He could not find the Guild of All Arts. A letter to Spencer stated that they would not, and did not, make deliveries so far out of the city. Someone would have to pick up this order and any future ones.

Dining Rooms: Top—Oak Dining Room
Bottom—Canary Dining Room

At that time Eglinton Avenue did not connect with the road allowance to the Guild because of the hill. Today this road is known as Guildwood Parkway.

An example of what staff and workers received is shown in the case of Paul J. K. Kneller who worked on landscaping. He lived at the Guild House and was given meals, articles of clothing, his laundry was done for him and received 50¢ a week in salary. If he was required to work for a longer period of time than first agreed to, he would be accommodated in a cabin. For this he had to trim, prune and clean from the gates along the roadway. There were ditches to be enlarged around the circular driveway as well as widening, leveling and crowning the private road. A stone pathway was to be constructed from the stonewall to the edge of the bluffs. These were a few of the things he was expected to do for the benefits he received.

One of the aims of the co-operative was to set up a teaching programme in the various crafts. There would be a full time craftsman and apprentices. This would train them for a career in weaving, woodworking, wrought iron and ceramics, to show these apprentices that they could use their skills as a profession rather than just for a hobby. Later leather tooling was included. Apprentices were expected to stay for a certain period of time and produce saleable goods. In this way the Guild operated small scale manufacturing. However, none of the crafts made a profit so the co-operative was a constant financial struggle.

The Guild of All Arts was advertised and written about in newspapers. Visitors flocked to see this unique venture and spent much of the day on the property. Rosa and Spencer began serving light refreshments to these visitors, afternoon tea, salads and sandwiches. Finally they decided that they should also be serving dinner. Miss Violet Reilly from Eaton's Georgian Room and Miss Leona Richardson, from Simpson's Arcadian Court, were two dietitians who helped set up the meals. In 1934-35, Spencer estimated they were serving 200–300 meals per day.

Finances were a huge problem and Rosa constantly worried about them. One time, Spencer explained in a letter to his brother-in-law, Paul Breithaupt, he was still up at 3:00 a.m. trying to figure out how he could find the money to put into the bank before several

Sleighing party—February 26, 1940
From the collection of The Guild

cheques were presented for payment. Spencer also mentioned the milk cheque. It had been put out with the empty bottles to pay their account. However, he had to retrieve this cheque and beat the milkman to it by about ten minutes. Then he asked Paul to send them $100.00 and $15.00 a week to help ease the crisis.

In the summertime meals brought in revenue, but during the winter months there were very few visitors. In December 1939, breakfast was served between 7:30–10:30 a.m., luncheon from 12:30–2:30 p.m., afternoon tea was served from 3:00–5:00 p.m. and dinner from 6:00–9:00 p.m. On Sundays and holidays, lunch was from 1:00–2:30 p.m. and dinner from 5:30 p.m. A dinner menu began with grapefruit juice, beef of Bouillon and saltines. For $1.25 the meal was beef tenderloin steak, red currant jelly or grilled lamb chops with bacon. Calves' liver sauteed with bacon cost $1.00. Vegetables were either parsley potatoes, buttered turnips or green peas. Dessert included five choices, deep custard pie, chantilly, baked apple with cream, chocolate ice box cake, or cheese with wafer. There was also hot homemade rolls. Beverages were tea, coffee and gingerale. The menu was typed on a yellow, half sheet of paper inside a border.

In November 1933 for an after-sleighing party Saturday evening, a group of 15 people would be charged 85¢ each. The menu included oyster stew with hot crisp crackers, hot cheese dreams, cinnamon toast, toast and honey and coffee. If the group stayed for dancing, for 25¢ more, they could have ice cream, cake and punch.

In 1933 another way to raise revenue was through a membership programme. For $8.00, a person could become an Associate Member with total access to the grounds, ten lectures and ten concerts. They could have tea for 30¢ each.

*"...There was only one dinner chef and he was not well paid. But the buns—oh the buns! For a few years during the 40s, a resident baker produced marvellous buns, crusty rolls, and sweet cinnamon buns that delighted the customers and staff..."*quote from Memories of David Pogue.

An American named Mr. Ferguson suggested that Rosa and Spencer add more guest rooms to become a country resort. However, they had to have recreational facilities which meant purchasing more property. Other lodges had between 500 to 1000 acres for activities such as golf courses, horseback riding, tobogganing and skiing. Rosa and Spencer began buying property from the area which is now Scarborough Golf Club Rd. to Galloway Rd., approximately 500 acres. It took them 30 years to complete the purchase of this property. They also added a third floor and Dr. Robert Jackson, whose property is now part of the Metro Zoo, a close friend and board member, helped with the financing. Guest accommodation proved to be more profitable than either the meals or the crafts.

On the second floor a two-room suite was established for a resident named Mrs. Mendel. Her husband was a wealthy textile manufacturer in Germany. Their only daughter married her cousin Dr. Bruno Mendel.

In Canada Dr. Frederick Banting was doing cancer research. He needed an associate and went to Europe to locate one. He invited Dr. Mendel to Canada to work with him. In 1930 when Mrs. Mendel's daughter moved to Canada with her husband, she also left Germany.

For awhile Mrs. Mendel lived in various hotels which she found unsatisfactory. One Sunday she visited the Guild Inn for brunch and loved the Inn and the country atmosphere. She wanted a lifetime lease but consented to a five year agreement. Her suite consisted of a vestibule, bathroom, bedroom and living room.

Frederick Banting was Spencer's friend and many times he visited Mrs. Mendel in her suite. Because of this, the room has been named after him. Mrs. Mendel's living room is the Banting room and the bedroom she used is now a storage room.

With added usage of water, the Inn began experiencing problems. In 1933 the Guild was without water for 1 1/2 weeks. Water had to be trucked in from neighbours and the city also helped. The Commissioner of the Street Cleaning Department, a close friend of Spencer's, sent five truck loads of 1000 gallons of water in their steel trucks. A study was made on where to find more water. Several wells were drilled to 80' depth but were dry.

A suggestion was made to pump water up from the lake. This was difficult to do. The shoreline was too narrow to build a pump house. It would need major construction to build an intake pipe and anchor it securely against damage from storms. Drainage from the cliffs would contaminate the water that would be pumped up for usage. Heavy horsepower engines would be necessary to pump the water up the cliffs and against the currents. This was not a plausible way to alleviate the water shortage problems.

A simple solution was located. There was a well the gardeners used that had plenty of water. This well was being fed by springs on higher levels north west of the building. In an old history of Scarborough dated 1896, published to commemorate the centenary, there was mention of some "healing wells" located along the south side of Eglinton Avenue (now Guildwood Parkway) east of Livingston Road. In this location there was at that time a dense bush of dogwood and soggy black soil. This was in a direct line with the well used for the market garden. On the Dart Farm, south of the highway (Kingston Rd.) springs of water ran out of the hill and across this property. Agreements had been made by Rosa and Spencer to have first rights to buy this property when they could afford the cost. They purchased the land and began drilling for water. They started drilling 100' back from each road and after several feet of soil, they struck clay. They moved the drilling closer to the roads, 10' back and drilled again. After less than 4' deep, they struck water. The main water source became five wells on the north west side of the property where Sir Wilfred Laurier Collegiate is. Hand pumps were first used to collect the water, then power pumps. The water flowed out strongly, it was clean, tasted good and seemed to be inexhaustible. Wells were created in the hill to collect water, then gravity- fed through pipes westward along the road allowance, across Livingston Rd. and across the Dart farm. These pipes fed the five wells.

Another problem was the erosion of the bluffs. Spencer tried various ways to stop the loss of property which was approximately 1.6 feet per year. He instituted controlled drainage a mile along the top of the bluffs by building shallow saucers 200' in diameter with edges raised to stop water going over the bluffs. The water was directed to drains, to manholes and to storm pipes.

In 1933 a neighbour had built a fishing dock east of the Guild which seemed to act as a groyne, a land stabilizer. Spencer saw how

Piano in the front hallway
From the collection of The Guild

effective this was for erosion control and built more along the frontage below the Guild. These were made from steel oil drums filled with sand and gravel, the open end plugged with concrete. However, the water level of the lake rose and the erosion began again. He towed steel barges from Toronto, Hamilton, Port Dalhousie, and anchored them at the foot of the cliffs. One wooden barge, purchased in 1955, was sunk in front of the property, and the 6' deep cavity filled with concrete and rocks. In 1967 he purchased a dry dock and positioned the hull in the water thereby widening the beach which slowed the erosion. He also trucked in 300,000 loads of excavated fill and masonry. This widened the beach and protected the cliffs from the waves.

David Pogue, son of Frank Pogue who was the business manager for several years, remembers an entertainer. "...In the early 40s a grand piano was placed in the hallway to entertain guests with dinner music...Cecil Barnum-Kappey, a pianist in his late 50s, who played dinner music...for about three years...He dressed in a jaunty, somewhat foppish way and smoked cigarettes from a holder...but how he could play!...He was pretentious, cynical person who had a steaming, lower-class hatred for the owner. He would steal things as a right and, in the safety of his (the owner's) absence, would tell the owner what to do with the Guild, brick by brick."

In 1948 guests coming by bus were met at Stop 29 on Kingston Rd. by the Guild Station Wagon, a Pontiac woody-wagon. The Inn could accommodate 102 guests on 400 acres containing 4 major buildings and 8 smaller ones. Taxis from the railway station, the bus depot or Canada Steamship Lines dock to the Inn cost $3.50.

The prime season was from May 1st to October 15th with different rates for the winter season. At this time there were three floors to the Inn. Room rates were based on the European plan—no meals. A single room without a bathroom cost $4.00 per day. Double rooms with double beds, and no bathroom, cost $6.00 or $7.00 depending on the room. Rooms with bathrooms and tiled floors, and double beds, the cost ranged from $8.00 to $12.00. At the same price there were also rooms with twin beds and bathrooms. For an extra $4.50 per day you could include meals. In 1952 rates had increased slightly to $14.00 for double rooms with a bathroom.

The Woody Wagon
From the collection of The Guild

A bedroom in the Guild Inn
From the collection of The Guild

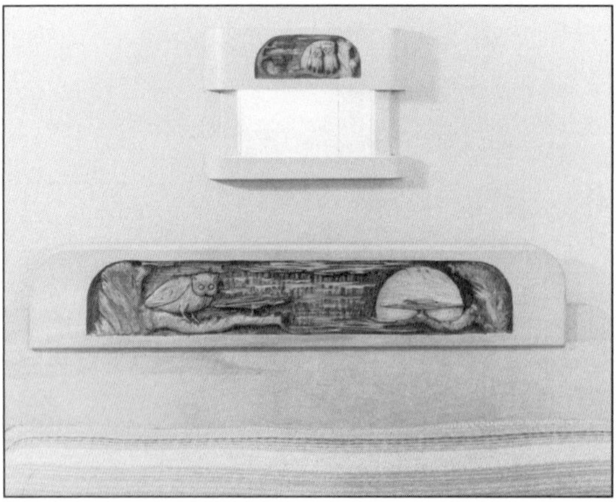

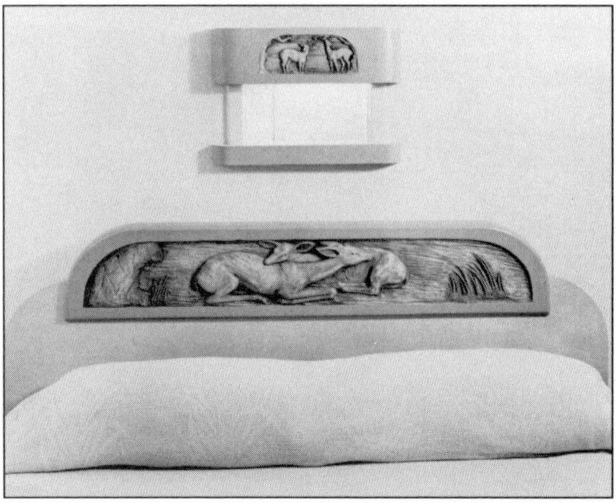

Bedroom Headboards
From the collection of The Guild

Each of the rooms had handmade furniture constructed by the craftsmen. Head boards were carved with different animals, birds and plants, by Aage Madsen or Alfred Perry, symbolizing Canadian wildlife.

In 1934 Rosa, Spencer, and the children, moved out of the main building, Guild House. The Inn had become so popular that they needed another place to call home. They purchased the property known as Corycliff and lived there for many years. Shortly before the Department of Veterans' Affairs took over the Guild property in 1940, the Clarks moved to 1 Dale Ave. and lived there for 26 years. In 1970 they moved to 33 Guildcrest Dr.

During WWII in 1943, the Guild Inn was used for training of a different type. The WRENS were located here for specialized wireless training (radio telegraphy) and it became known as HMSC Bytown II. The Guild of All Arts tried to operate as usual but the craftsmen had signed up for military service so there was less work being done.

During the war, material for the crafts were also unavailable. The fancy yarns for weaving disappeared. Restrictions were placed on the sale of steel and iron. The ornamental iron work was discontinued and the wrought iron department was closed. The main source for tin came from the South Pacific, the Marlee Peninsula. After the attack on Pearl Harbour by the Japanese, this material became unavailable. Pewter, which was a material being used at the Guild, was 90% tin, so could no longer be obtained. The Guild bought large quantities of copper to keep that department going through the war. Six months later they were visited by a government inspector who had copies of all their invoices. The copper was taken from the Guild and shipped to a munitions plant in Ajax, Ontario. The copper department then had to be closed. Gas was also rationed and guests were restricted from driving to the Guild. Other items rationed were butter, flour and meat.

As well, during this time delegations of Generals, Admirals and Air Force Officers paid unannounced visits. The result was that the Guild became a hospital for war veterans with shattered nerves. This was administered by the Christie Street Hospital in Toronto.

In 1947 Rosa and Spencer regained occupation of the Guild. In March 1947 they began three months of intensive work to re-open the Guild Inn and the Guild of All Arts.

The WRENS

Postcard of Uniformed WREN
From the collection of Mrs. Beverley J. Covington

Women's Royal Canadian Naval Service

"The Wrens"—October 1942 – May 1943

During World War II Spencer received a telephone call with a request to house a group of 50 women. These women had been trained in Galt, Ontario, to relieve naval men of shore duty. They called themselves WRENS. Two days after the telephone call, a convoy of trucks and lorries arrived at the Inn transporting the 50 WRENS.

These women had completed their basic training and were moved from Galt, Ontario to allow more women to be trained. Guildwood Hall was used by the WRENS and the locks on the doors were changed because of the secrecy of their work. They were housed in the main building, the Inn, and were provided with meals and recreational activities. During their occupation, the woodworking and weaving departments at the Inn were still in operation.

In Canada during World War II, 6000 women trained as WRENS. The training location in Galt, Ontario was first named HMCS Bytown (because Ottawa was once called Bytown) then it became HMCS Conestoga. When the WRENS were located at the Guild Inn, it was called HMCS Bytown II.

Frances Gage, a sculptor who worked at the Guild Inn for a short time, was once a WREN. In 1972 she created a sculpture to honour the WRENS which is located at the Library and Gallery in Cambridge, Ontario. That section of Cambridge was once Galt, Ontario.

Although the WRENS were part of the Navy, they never served on ships. It was still considered unlucky to have women on board, a superstition retained through the centuries by sailors. WRENS were organized to serve only for land-based duties doing office work and intelligence gathering. To assist in setting up a training programme, three senior officers arrived from the British WRENS in England.

These officers selected the first 67 recruits from across Canada and training began at Kingsmill House in Ottawa, Ontario. Twenty-two of these recruits became officers and a short time later 2000 young Canadian women had enlisted as WRENS.

WREN Statue in Cambridge, Ontario
From the collection of the author

In Galt, Ontario, at the Grandview School for Girls, a training centre was established. The first recruits were women from the professional fields of business, education, science and politics. Training lasted four weeks in the atmosphere of a regular naval barracks. The recruits had marching drills, attended lectures, scrubbed decks, made beds, peeled potatoes and washed dishes. In an article by June Breece a recruit stated:

"...The ship was a former school for delinquent girls...They blew whistles for everything...we scrubbed that ship from top to bottom...we polished brass...were lectures, including all the terrible things that could happen to you, like venereal diseases."

Another recruit said, "*...we have to act just as if we were sailors in a ship...*"

The only naval uniform issued to these first recruits was a short-sleeved, navy blue cotton smock. Later they were issued a tailored uniform consisting of white shirts, dark ties, navy blue jackets and skirts, with black stockings and shoes. Their first hats were a floppy pork-pie style which looked like a nursing sister's hat. This was soon replaced with hats of blue similar to those worn by the regular navy. Officers wore tri-corn hats. During the summer the uniform was light blue.

After basic training the WRENS were sent elsewhere to learn wireless telegraphy, coding, teletyping and radar. The training lasted fourteen weeks, taught to them by a male, and the WRENS learned semaphore, flag hoists and Morse code. Some of them were sent to Naval bases across Canada as writers, supply assistants, sick berth attendants, drivers, dietitians, sailmakers, switchboard operators, just to name a few of the thirty-nine trades opened to them. An overseas positing of 586 WRENS went to Newfoundland.

The women who joined the WRENS had to be, and show, that they were ladies. They worked with secret information, secret codes, signalled convoys with warnings about enemy U-boats, and worked in monitoring stations on the east coast. In July 1946 the WRENS were officially disbanded until 1954 when a permanent force was created.

Today the WRENS longer a separate group of women in the navy known as WRENS. They became part of the regular navy when the three services, Army, Navy and Airforce, amalgamated into one group by the Canadian Government.

Scarborough Hall—Recuperative Centre 1944–1947

In England there was a unique hospital called Mill Hill which was for patients with nervous disorders. In Toronto the Christie Street Hospital for veterans could no longer provide decent care. The head of the Canadian Council of Mental Hygiene, Dr. Clarence Finks, went to England to evaluate the operation of Mill Hill Hospital. The Canadian government was then persuaded to create a similar hospital in Canada. The Superintendent from Mill Hill Hospital toured Canada to locate a suitable place to open this type of hospital. He decided that the Guild Inn was the perfect location.

The relaxing atmosphere of the Guild Inn, its extensive property and magnificent view, were aspects beneficial to healing neuro-psychic disorders. There were facilities for the patients to work on various crafts and do their own gardening. The Guild Inn was also in a secluded location but still close to the city for easy transportation of the patients. Unfortunately this meant that the Guild's own activities would have to close, all except the woodworking department.

In 1944 the government took over the Guild Inn and called its new hospital, Scarborough Hall. One hundred patients at a time could be accommodated here for a few weeks or months. Alterations enabled a capacity of 200 patients to be accommodated at one time. Guildwood Hall was also used and accommodated 30 patients.

Scarborough Hall was leased by the Department of Pensions and National Health for $21,000.00 per year. This remained in effect until 1947.

Earlier in 1942, public-spirited women forced the government to consider better hospitalization for returning war veterans. A committee was formed, the Greater Toronto Veterans Hospital Committee, to select a suitable site. The city offered a farm they had acquired in 1928, Sunnybrook Farm. In 1944, on Remembrance Day, the cornerstone was laid for a neuropschiatry hospital, Sunnybrook. In 1946, after delays from a shortage of labourers and material, while construction continued, patients were admitted. Scarborough Hall, in 1947, once again became the Guild Inn. Christie Street Hospital later became a municipally-owned nursing home.

A Craftsman's Creed

I hold with none who think not work a boon. Vouchsafed to man that he may aid his kind. With offerings from his chisel, wheel or loom, fashioned with loving heart and loving mind. All of the fine traditions and the skill, came from my elders through the long line down, are mine to use to raise our craft's renown. And mine to teach again with reverent will. Thus do I live to serve, though least for pay, with fingers which are masters of the tool and eyes which light to see the patterns play. As it unfolds obedient to each rule of our dear art. So all my craft is praise to God—at once part homage and part song. My work's my prayer. I sing the whole day long as faith and beauty shape the forms I raise.

Weaving

William Dawson operating the 100" loom
From the collection of The Guild

The Guild of All Arts—Weaving

During the years of the colony of artists and craftsmen, 30,000 portable weaving looms were built, sold and shipped to all parts of the world. It is estimated that well over 10,000 people were taught to weave on these hand looms. Mrs. Grace Poque was one of the teachers who held classes at the Guild of All Arts.

A 100" wide loom, believed to be Canada's largest hand-loom, was designed and built at the Guild. On the wall in the hallway of the Guild Inn is a large black and white photograph of William Dawson operating the large loom. It contained 16 frames of heddle-harness (a heddle is a series of bars—each with a hole and a slot—to hold the strands of yarn), plus a Jacquard mechanism (a fabric of intricate variegated weave or pattern). There were warp beams (holding the lengthwise threads on a loom) for double weaving, and flying shuttles (an instrument for passing the horizontal threads between the vertical threads).

Some items produced on these looms were used in the Inn. Bedspreads in the guest rooms were hand-woven on these looms by weavers, William Dawson, Margaret Hartwell, Kathleen Hunt, Alex McDowell and Grace Poque. Many weaving students also contributed to the items that were used and sold. Several rooms of the Inn, the Upper Oak and Coral dining room, displayed the weavers' work. Material woven from jute prairie binder twine, which lasted more than 49 years, was glued to the walls then painted and varnished. Draperies and upholstery, woven on the looms were used in the Inn. Other products were hand bags, purses, scarves and pile rugs to name just a few. During the great depression this weaving was to help the weavers earn a living from their work.

From 1938 to 1943 a shop at 44 Bloor Street West sold products made at the Guild. As well, Simpson's department store, for a month, displayed Guild looms and hand woven suiting. Other stores were also pleased to put these items on display. In co-operation with Monarch Knitting, the 100" loom was displayed in 1935 at the C.N.E. (Canadian National Exhibition) and in the Guild's own booth.

L to R: Rosemary, Dorothy, Ruth Hewetson
From the Breithaupt Hewetson Clark Collection
University of Waterloo

Other people who benefited from weaving instructions were the blind from the C.N.I.B. (Canadian Institute for the Blind), as well as students from several deaf schools in Brantford and Belleville.

Rosa and her three daughters, Rosemary, Ruth and Dorothy, were involved in weaving material for their own clothes. An article in the Globe & Mail, February 2, 1938, mentions that in one day Rosa had created material for a new skirt. In the morning she began weaving a bright plaid material. By noon the weaving was finished. For buttons she asked artisans in the workshop to create circles which were hammered out of pewter. In their spare hours, over a period of four days, Rosemary, Ruth and Dorothy, on a 30" Utility Loom, wove 71/2 yards of material for each of their winter coats. A competition at the C.N.E. for handwoven army, navy or air force scarves was won by 15 year old Rosemary. A scarf could be completed in about 2 hours.

Mrs. Grace Poque was also a winning weaver. At the C.N.E. in August 1941, in her second year of entering her work, she won eight prizes out of nine entries. The previous year she won six prizes.

In 1989, upstairs in Guildwood Hall, there was an inventory taken of the weaving looms. [1]

Guildcraft Loomex Loom 6"–2 packaged
Guildcraft Loomex Loom 9"–2 packaged

Junior A	- 1 assembled (parts missing)
Junior B	- 2 packaged (parts missing from each)
	- 1 assembled
Speed Loom	- 12"–1 packaged
	- 2 assembled
Speed Loom	- 16"–1 packaged
22" Loom	- 2 packaged (parts missing from each)
	- 4 assembled
30" Loom	- 2 packaged
	- 1 assembled

1 *In 1999 I toured the second floor and discovered that the 100" loom still exists although it is covered with dust instead of weaving threads. There were also spinning wheels and smaller looms in various sizes.*

Postcard of the Weaving Studio
From the collection of The Guild

English and Canadians experimented with weaving looms to try to put a simple loom in every home. The Guild Inn was involved in the evolution of this new style of loom. In 1936 Rosa and Spencer visited Mrs. Thackery in England. The three of them spent many weeks improving the design of the loom developed by William Thackery. Rosa and Spencer purchased the distribution rights for Canada, the United States and Britain. At the Guild Inn Spencer combined the principles of the Thackery Loom with his own ideas to create the Silent Speed Loom.

With each loom there were instructions on its use and patterns for weaving for example, the *"Rose Path, Honeysuckle, Orange Peel, Chariot Wheels and Monks Belt*." There were also instructions for special weaves such as the *"Guild Special Suiting Weave*."

The 15" Utility Loom, equipped with four heddle bars, sold for $21.50. The 22" loom for wider, longer and heavier weaving, cost $29.50. Henry Ford of Dearborn, Michigan, ordered a 12" Silent Speed Loom at a cost of $12.50.

Frank Pogue—Business Manager
From the personal collection of son David Pogue

Frank and Grace Pogue

Frank Pogue was born in New Westminster, B.C. to a poor Irish family who had migrated from the area of Haliburton, Ontario so his father, a harness maker, could find a market for his product. Due to harsh treatment from his father, he left home before completing high school. He completed his education through correspondence while learning the trade of a watchmaker. His sketching, calligraphy, typing and shorthand got him a job with the Home Bank in Alberta. In 1921 Frank married a widow, Grace, with two sons whose first husband had also been named Pogue. Eight years later a third son, David was born. Each of them worked at the Guild Inn. During the 1930s he was employed at the Guild of All Arts as their Business Manager.

Frank joined the Royal Air Force and was transferred to the Toronto area. He flew experimental aircraft and some of his friends crashed and died in these planes. A crash Frank was involved with only knocked out several of his teeth. After the war he studied advertising and public speaking, commercial and public relations in Toronto.

As well as managing the Guild, Frank used his other skills. He was also a photographer. Frank designed a placemat used in the dining rooms. His marketing skills were used to promote the weaving looms and develop customer relations. Unfortunately, his association with the Guild lasted for only two years.

The staff could not be paid their wages. The Guild was on the verge of bankruptcy and Frank had a family to support. He was then hired to work in the Membership and Publicity Department of the Toronto Board of Trade.

Grace Pogue learned weaving at the Guild then taught and demonstrated weaving on the Guild looms. These looms were set up at the back of the shop which was in a room at the front of the inn, to the left of the main entrance. Grace was an award-winning weaver at the C.N.E. Weaving was her hobby which she taught to invalids and elderly people. Some of her pupils also had winning entries.

Grace and Frank Pogue
From the personal collection of David Pogue

Rolph Pogue, the second son, remembers sleeping in the cabin near the barn which stabled a horse that he wanted to ride. He climbed on and was promptly thrown off. Later, this same horse ran away then was struck and killed by a train.

Spencer Clark owned a Studebaker and a Pierce Arrow, the latter driven once by Ralph. He drove Rosa to Georgian Bay and spent time in her island cottage.

The youngest son, David, remembers his mother and himself living with the Clark family in Corycliff for several summers. He enjoyed sitting in the screened porch, and was fascinated by the electric storms on Lake Ontario. He climbed an old apple tree, and enjoyed sitting in another tree with limbs hanging out over the bluffs.

The tiny office where waitresses settled bills, and hotel guests checked in or out, fascinated him. A typewriter in the office was used to type up the next day's menu onto sand-coloured stationery. He remembers typing some of these menus.

Grace Pogue died in 1965, and the year before, Frank had died of a heart attack. Rolph, 80 years old in 1998, and David almost 70, have fond memories of their time at the Guild Inn. The eldest son, Robert, died a few years earlier.

"The Guild was an important part of my youth and it provided a very significant piece of my family's history," said David Pogue.

Grace Pogue Weaving at one of the Guild's Looms
From the collection of David Pogue

Sculpture

Sculptor working at the Sculpture Cabin
From the collection of sculptor Tom Feenstra

The Scultpure Studio

In 1940 Aage Madsen, a Danish wood sculptor, built the Sculpture Studio on the grounds of the Guild of All Arts. In its early years it was painted with bright colours which have faded to warm brown, and natural wood. The door is split, so the top portion can be opened while the bottom remains closed. A fireplace against the back wall has two soot-streaked bats on the mantelpiece[1], which is the only source of heating. At one time there were carvings which were stolen. In 1979 Dorsey James was commissioned to create new carvings. The carvings represent Norse mythology from the Volsunga Saga. Along the eaves is a carving of the dragon Fafnir, killed by the warrior Sigurd. On the left side of the door, usually in the sunlight, the warrior head is that of Sigurd. On the right side, usually shadowed from the sun, is the warrior Regin. The sword beside the window represents the one that Loki used to kill the otter which had caused trouble between the warriors in search of a treasure.

In 1987 the sculpture cabin required numerous repairs. The roof leaked which affected the lights and fuses were frequently blowing. All around the roof, under the eaves, dry rot had set in. The walls of the building needed a coat of stain to preserve the building. In 1988 the Board of Management passed a motion due to the disrepair of the studio.

> *"..the Metro owned building known as the Sculpture Studio not be used as a public reception area and sculpture exhibition space on November 26, 1988 nor at any time until further notice."*

---

1 *Letter from Tom Feenstra, January 20, 1991*

Apparently, no money was available for repairs to the building. Dorsey James offered to do the repairs but was not allowed to do so. In 1994 the studio was the victim of vandalism, again! Several of the windows had been broken. Sections of the shelves had been burned in the fireplace. The north and north-west windows, on the inside, were then boarded up with plywood panels to prevent further unwarranted entries.

In 2000 the Sculpture Studio stands empty and unused. Hopefully one day it will once again become the working space for sculptors.

Thomas Bowie—Sculptor
1905–1996

"I tried to instill some new life in the college. Teaching is a challenge. You teach the basic ideas and leave it open for interpretations." —Thomas Bowie

Thomas Bowie came to Canada to apply for a job because his wife Betty insisted he go. She had seen an announcement from the Ontario College of Arts looking for a sculptor for a new course. Thomas worked in Scotland for a well-known sculptor, Pilkington Jackson and as an apprentice and assistant, all his work was credited to Pilkington. His wife Betty thought it was time he received credit for his work and urged him to apply for the job in Canada. He applied and was accepted.

In 1953 he moved to Canada but left his wife Betty and five children in Scotland. He wanted to make sure that the job would last before uprooting them. In later years he became the director of the sculpture department of the O.C.A.

Thomas Bowie was born in Linlithgow, Scotland to shoemaker Robert Bowie and his wife, a domestic servant. At sixteen he began an apprenticeship under Pilkington Jackson. At age 19, he came to Canada to work on a sculpture in Toronto, a bronze cenotaph. He made the models for the cenotaph in Toronto. He then returned to Scotland for further studies under Pilkington.

One of the sculptures he was requested to do was a bust of Princess Elizabeth. For this sculpture he worked in their home and was escorted in and our by guardsmen. Although he created the work, the credit was given to Pilkington Jackson.

Thomas married Betty Bell and they had three sons and two daughters. When he moved to Canada, and later brought Betty, their youngest son Alan came too. Their first home was on Lynnvalley Crescent in Scarborough. Betty became a housekeeper at the Guild Inn.

Sculptor Thomas Bowie and poet Wallace Havelock Robb
From the collection of The Guild

Rosa Clark took sculpture lessons at an evening course at the Ontario College of Art from Thomas Bowie. She enquired if he was related to their housekeeper, Betty Bowie, which led to him being invited to work at the Guild Inn. A house was available at 18 Woodvale Road next to the Inn and the Bowie family moved into it. Their daughter, Margaret, joined them in Canada.

Thomas worked in the Sculpture Cabin and was commissioned by Rosa to do a special piece. On the grounds of the Inn was a section where Rosa's, and the children's, pets were buried. She wanted a sculpture to identify this location. He used his son Alan and his dog Blackie as a model for the sculpture of St. Francis of Assisi and a wolf. Blackie was later buried in the Guild's pet cemetery.

At the Guild Inn, In 1956, Tom had an exhibit of his work, many of the items borrowed from private collections. The sculptures were a torso carved from Carrera marble; a frolicsome horse carved from maple wood; a maiden dressing her hair carved from chestnut wood, to name a few of the items. The wife of Rosa's son Russell, loaned a terra cotta stone carving of Jonah and the whale. The model for this sculpture, owned by his daughter Margaret, is a unique design. An open outline of the whale, shows Jonah trapped inside, one style that Tom often employed. He opened up his design, such as the "crazy horse" he did for a school, and shows inside details such as ribs.

The St. Francis of Assisi sculpture was dedicated on September 30, 1956, at the opening of the exhibit. Lorne Pierce gave the dedication and a talk on the sculpture. "...Today we dedicate this impressive and reverent interpretation of St. Francis and the wolf by the distinguished sculptor, Mr. Thomas Bowie. It will stand here, in these lovely gardens, as a perpetual pledge, that Truth and Beauty shall walk hand in hand with Goodness, and Compassion...We are told that when wolves preyed upon a village he banished them simply by the power of his vast love for all living things...a fierce wolf...was tamed by his love, became his companion and protector..."

In 1961 Tom returned to Scotland to work on a sculpture of Robert the Bruce, a Scottish hero, for Pilkington Jackson. Credit for the 18 foot high equestrian statue that Pilkington was too old to work on, was not received by its creator, Thomas Bowie.

Thomas Bowie with his sculpture of St. Francis of Assisi
From the personal collection of Margaret Beckman (daughter)

Material Tom liked to use were stone, plaster, marble, wood, metal and bronze. One material was fibreglass resin, mostly used for car repairs. He made wire-mesh forms then covered them with the resin. Most often he used this for making models but several larger sculptures are made from this. In Brampton, at the Shopper's World Mall, stands his resin-coated statue of a family group. At the Inn on the Park Hotel is his abstract model of a horse. To make these sculptures look like bronze, he often used the shavings from cutting keys to create that appearance.

Tom liked his work to look natural. He usually did sculptures that were realistic except when he did horses. They always had a fanciful aspect.

For a camp in Sundridge, Ontario, he created a tall totem pole which was seen by a girl from British Columbia who attended the camp and loved this work. When she returned home her father commissioned Tom to create a totem pole for her. A tree was shipped from British Columbia, and when completed, was shipped back in a greatly altered state.

One of Tom's students working on religions icons for All Saints Church in Bermuda, died suddenly. He was asked to complete the work there because she had used his methods. While completing this work, Tom was housed as a guest of the Governor of Bermuda.

In Scarborough when Guildwood Hall was replaced by a high school, Tom was commissioned to do a bust of the school's namesake, Sir Wilfred Laurier, which still stands in this school. One of the busts he created in the Sculpture Cabin was of Elvis Presley, done mostly from photographs. Elvis did come for one sitting.

He made a living from his art, which included teaching at the Ontario College of Art. However, he chose not to use galleries to sell his work which would have increased the price. Instead he sold his work to private collectors and through the Sculptor's Society.

The family later moved to 11 Morna Drive when Guildwood Village was developed. Tom's garage became his studio where he also gave lessons and he continued working in the Sculpture Cabin year round. Unfortunately, he had a disagreement with a maintenance man.

During the winter the maintenance man plowed the snow up against the cabin. Tom had to shovel his way in. Someone on the staff complained that this was not good for visitors and the man was told to discontinue this practice.

He and Betty returned several times to live in Scotland but always returned to Canada. When Tom's wife, Betty, died in May 1985, he moved to Sunderland, Ontario. His arthritis prevented him from working with heavy materials so he used the fibreglass resin and began painting with watercolour and oil paints. Later he moved to Cobourg where his children Alan and Margaret live. Tom received the Centennial Medal for his sculptures and work at the base of the Oneida Tower in Niagara Falls. He died on January 27, 1996, was cremated and his ashes buried in Memorial Gardens.

Alan remembers as a child when he didn't complete his climb up the clay bluffs. He broke his leg and had to be rescued. His worry was for his new leopard skin bathing suit. He didn't want his rescuers to cut it.

Margaret worked in the office and then in the kitchen. She met her husband at the Guild Inn and was married with the reception in the Studio building.

John Robert Monk Byers—Sculptor 1905–1972

Paul Breithaupt, younger brother of Rosa, requested a sculpture of Robert Holmes, a famous Canadian painter of wild flowers. He asked John Byers to create this work which was unveiled in 1938 on the location called "Abby Down", near Kingston, Ontario, a property owned by poet Wallace Havelock Robb. In 1962 this sculpture was donated to the Guild Inn when the wildlife sanctuary was closed.

John Byers was born in Brockville, Ontario and studied landscape painting at the Ontario College of Art. He studied sculpture at Central Technical School under teacher Emanuel Hahn.

In 1928 he received a special mention in the Governor General's competition. In 1940, while living in Fort William, Ontario (now part of Thunder Bay) he became the founding president of the Fort William Society of Art. Moving to Montreal, Quebec he became a teacher at Lachine High School, teaching sculpture and metal work. He retired in 1968 and in retirement taught sculpture at the Guild Inn.

Sculptor E.B. Cox at home
From the author's collection

E.B. Cox—Sculptor
1914

At age 84 E. B. Cox has hundreds of sculptures displayed in public places in Toronto and other areas. At the C.N.E. twenty of his creations called the Garden of the Greek Gods are located in front of the Horticulture Building, attract attention and children love to climb over them. In June Ardiel's *Sculpture/Toronto: An Illustrated Guide to Toronto's Historic and Contemporary Sculpture*, it states that E. B. Cox has more sculpture on view in Toronto than any other single sculptor. One of his pieces is located at the Guild Inn and was done in 1979 in collaboration with Michael Clay. It is a large white bear made from Portland limestone, standing 56" high. Because it is white visitors view this as a replica of a polar bear, but it's a black bear. E. B. said, "...polar bears have a distinct structure...a different leg structure, a different snoot, and different neck structure..."

E. B. Cox, who uses his initials as other artists such as A.Y. Jackson have done, commented "...never ask a sculptor how long it takes to create a sculpture...I have no idea how long it took (to create a sculpture in his home done two months ago)...I have no memory of doing it...and yet it was done. I recognize my work."

He was born in Alberta on July 16, 1914 and educated at the University of Toronto in modern languages. For eleven years he taught French and German at Upper Canada College. During WWII he served 3½ years in the armed forces and returned to teaching until 1950 when he became a full-time sculptor. He met Spencer Clark during the 1960s when Spencer bought some of his pieces for his private collection.

E. B. said "...Spencer was a gentleman and he liked to encourage people and he helped them on their way selflessly. He bought things...and provided a home for Michael Clay for years."

The material E. B. used range from sumac wood, limestone and alabaster. Other materials were serpentine, onyx, granite, marble, cedar wood, and walnut. "...There are 300 kinds of marble...some are hard and some are soft...some are brittle and some are no good." E. B. enjoys doing bears of all shapes and sizes chipping them from stone and wood. He works from a studio at his home and said,

E.B. Cox and his native masks
From the author's collection

"...it's hard to get studio space especially with the noisy business of stone carving, dusty and noisy with an air compressor."

E.B. prices his sculptures according to what the public will pay. A small sculpture of pink alabaster[1] is a finely chiseled face of a sleeping, or dreaming woman, her hair flowing out behind her head. He creates quickly, completing a small piece within a few hours and is able to make a comfortable living from his work. "...I invented unimportant sculptures...I invented nice little things at reasonable prices...that can be lifted and dusted around (on a coffee table) and I sold them...one thing after another...you just have to do good things." Today he sells his pieces by word of mouth. For sixteen years he sold his work through Roberts Gallery and other small galleries. Various private collectors purchase his work directly from him.

In his home, Haida mask faces, some vividly painted, stare down from the walls. "...west coast is the most evident, primitive art in the world. I saw them as a child and was able to carve them quite casually." He no longer has the pieces he carved in childhood. He uses pictures from books as designs for his masks. "...I study it and say what is the quality...why is it so good?" Most of the masks are made from one piece of pine wood.

E. B. likes images from nature—bears, birds. "...I've carved hundreds of bears." He also likes people-related images, heads, bodies, torsos and hands. "...I don't carve from a model...because I don't make people I make statues...I try to make them look noble and good...I'm not interested in ugliness."

When the sculptures are completed sometimes E.B. feels very proprietary toward them and "...certain things I've had for 50-60 years...I can't live without them." He's been offered large sums of money for these pieces but they are not for sale.

In an article from Toronto Life Magazine, September 1997, William Gilpin describes E. B. Cox as "*...more than a sculptor...a successful paradox...creative and pragmatic, gentle and piquant, atheistic yet unwittingly spiritual, he revels in complexity.*"

---

1 *Author purchased it for $20.00*

Dorothy Dick—Sculptor

Dorothy Dick was an English sculptor married to artist Stewart Dick. In 1926 they visited Toronto, Ontario, Victoria and Vancouver, British Columbia, where Stewart was lecturing. The Toronto Daily Star, May 1, 1926 wrote an article about her. In it they quoted her as saying, "I always modeled since I was a child. I used to get pastry from the kitchen and make doll houses out of it." In 1932 and 1933 Dorothy was the resident sculptor at the Guild of All Arts.

Dorothy studied under the great English sculptor, Albert Gilbert, who would not allow her to attend an art school. He had noticed her talent when her father showed him something she had created. Instead of art school, he taught her himself.

At age 18 Dorothy received a commission to do a portrait of a member of parliament. She never met this member and had to do the work, a relief in silver (a sculpture in which the figures stand out from the flat surface), from photographs. For this she received £5 (five pounds—English money).

To make plaster extremely hard, Dorothy invented a process which also added colour. She used a mixture of gums and waxes, heated them together and then let the mixture run into the plaster. She was asked by the Victoria Albert Museum to sell them this process. Instead, she gave them the formula.

An article in the Toronto Daily Star describes Dorothy's clothing. At the time of the interview she was wearing a "...reddish sort of tam, drawn down to one side, in the true, nonchalant fashion of the preoccupied artist...her shoes? Nothing so dainty; they were boots. Russian boots or something simulating them. Dorothy Dick struck one as a woman at all times ready to sit down to her work..."

> "*You are not going to make a lifelike thing on a rigid piece of wood...*"

In the busts she created, Dorothy used lead piping as a core so she could tilt the head to portray it more naturally.

In October 1926, Dorothy and her husband had a joint showing of their work in the T. Eaton Company Art Salon. Dorothy displayed two busts, a girl titled "Reverie" and one of a young boy. Several coloured reliefs were displayed, one a Ukelele player and the Dancer. Stewart displayed forty water colours, some created in the Rocky mountains.

The Eaton family commissioned a plaque from Dorothy and she also created a Beaverbrook plaque. A bust she did of Hector Charlesworth was given to the Toronto Arts and Letters Club.

Dorothy and Stewart had one daughter, Margot, who is believed to have married a titled English gentleman.

Sculptor Sorel Etrog
From the collection of The Guild

Sorel Etrog—Sculptor
1933

Spencer Clark immediately recognized the talent of Sorel Etrog. In 1966 Spencer purchased a 50" high sculpture entitled "Moses." Many of Sorel's sculptures were in the Guild Inn's gardens.

Sorel was born in 1933 in Jassy, Romania. In 1950 he moved to Tel Aviv, Israel where he worked at various jobs. He was employed in a medical supply house from 1953 until 1956, and also served with the Israeli Army Medical Core. During this time he was studying at the Institute of Painting and Sculpture in Israel.

He began with painting but soon moved on to painted wood construction. In 1958 he had a one-man show which led to a scholarship at the Brooklyn Museum of Art in New York, U.S.A. His work is noted for forms that twist, curl and loop upwards.

Life was not easy in New York as Sorel could not speak English very well. His scholarship funds were inadequate and his art was not appreciated by American art dealers. Canadian art patrons, Samuel and Ayala Zacks, recognized his talent and invited him to Toronto, and to spend the summer of 1959 on Lake Huron. That same year, Walter Moos of Toronto gave him a one-man show which consisted of wood construction and paintings. In 1960 Sorel began exhibiting bronze sculptures.

Sorel set up a studio in Toronto in 1961. He settled permanently there in 1963 but spends time in Florence, Italy and Paris, France at his other studios. In 1965 the Director of the Toronto Art Gallery said about him, "...his work...a tendency to combine free curving lines with geometric shapes..." In 1966 Sorel was chosen as one of three artists to represent Canada at the Venice Biennial.

Sorel is a book illustrator as well as a sculptor. In 1967, for Claude Aveline in Montreal, he illustrated the book "*The Bird Which Does Not Exist*". Then in 1969 he illustrated the book *"Chocs"* by Ionesco.

In 1981 Spencer Clark commissioned him to create "The Space Plough" for the Guild Inn which is located in the north garden. For the 50th anniversary of the Inn, Spencer asked Sorel to organize an outdoor exhibition of contemporary sculpture. "More than half of the 35 artists created works specially for this exhibition..." The exhibition was held from August to October 1982, and a book of photographs and artist information was published for the event. "Solstice" by Kosso Eloul still stands in the garden as a reminder of this exhibition.

Sorel was an honourary pallbearer at the funeral of Rosa and also of Spencer. When Spencer died in 1986, Sorel wrote a tribute to him. He said about Spencer, "...He was a man of many dimensions...He loved sculpture..."

Sorel still has a studio in Toronto but has removed several of his sculptures, which were on loan, from the Guild Inn gardens.

Sculptor Michael Clay—lived in one of the cabins
From the collection of The Guild

Sculptor Tom Feenstra
From the author's collection

Tom Feenstra—Painter and Sculptor

January 1984
Thoughts on the Guild Inn
"...it brings people, who would seldom if ever go to a sculpture exhibition, in close contact with sculpture. It offers them the possibility to observe sculpture being created. There are always some finished pieces to show, some pieces that are being worked on, some raw material. The atmosphere is informal and relaxed inviting people to question and discover. Working together with Dorsey James, as a team, each on our own pieces, sharing ideas, discussing problems, has been a great experience. We co-operate rather than compete. Throughout the years we have established a rapport based on mutual respect that is now being recognized. The intensive use that we make of the Sculpture Studio during three of the four seasons, has helped to make the Guild more than just a pleasant hotel and convention centre. Our presence at the studio has attracted outside people to the Guild, people who after they have had their fill of the studio, head out to investigate what else the Guild has to offer...In winter I work in a basement four levels underground, concrete walls, no windows, plastic lights, stale air. I slowly die! In early spring I move back to the Guild and come rapidly back to life. The atmosphere and environment are stimulating and have a positive influence on my work."

Tom Feenstra was born in The Hague, Holland and trained in Amsterdam for the Merchant Navy. He choose this career because he wanted "to see the world" and use these experiences in his painting. However, working on ships did not allow him time to visit the places where he stopped. He left the Merchant Navy and worked at various jobs in the countries he travelled to.

Rome, Paris, Vienna, India, Indonesia, were places Tom stayed and worked, most often for one year. From Hong Kong he went to Japan and lived there for almost nine years. In Tokyo he taught music and learned to play the Shakuhachi, a Japanese instrument. He had to learn to read Japanese as well as speak it, as the music was written in Japanese characters. He also taught English as another part-time job.

Tom Feenstra and Dorsey James in the Sculpture Cabin
From the personal collection of Tom Feenstra

Then he felt the need for open spaces and in 1975 emigrated to Canada.

Earlier in his travels, he spent three years off and on in Spain while working in Holland. He learned to play Flamenco music on a guitar adding to his musical abilities.

In Canada recycling was being promoted and Tom thought he could do something with the pieces of wood he saw lying around. This is when he began sculpting, but kept painting as well. Then in 1980 he was one of the sculptors who created the maypole at Harbourfront in Toronto, Ontario.

Unfortunately for this group of sculptors, the city of Toronto wanted the maypole but didn't want to pay for the work. This maypole, with seven whales on it, still stands at Harbourfront. There is no plaque about the sculpture, sculptors nor the story behind it. Making a living as a sculptor was an impossibility, he needed to find a job.

The Guild Inn hired him as a houseman and here he met Dorsey James who was the sculptor in residence in the cabin. Dorsey introduced Tom to the use of power tools to create sculptures easier from wood. "...with wood you start with a solid block and you take away pieces...if the tools slip the sculpture is destroyed."

In 1988 they went their separate ways. At this time Tom began experiencing problems with arthritis. He gave up sculpting and continued with painting. "..painting is easy...if you don't like it you can remove the painting and you still have the canvas..."

Tom loves the shape of the violin and after taking lessons to play, without great success, incorporates the shape into his paintings. Paintings are done with acrylics, oil paints or dye, whatever the idea calls for. Tom has many ideas and inspiration for his paintings can come, for example, from watching clouds in the sky.

In 1990 he approached the Guild Inn curator about using the Sculpture Studio for painting. He'd heard that the cabin needed rewiring before it could be used, and he offered to pay $2,000.00 to have it done. In December 1990 he received a reply that there were plans to relocate the cabin and his offer was declined. He said in a reply letter to the curator, "...Things were simpler when Spencer was alive...Many plans have floated around since Spencer's death...but little has been done..." Tom requested the use of the cabin until it was

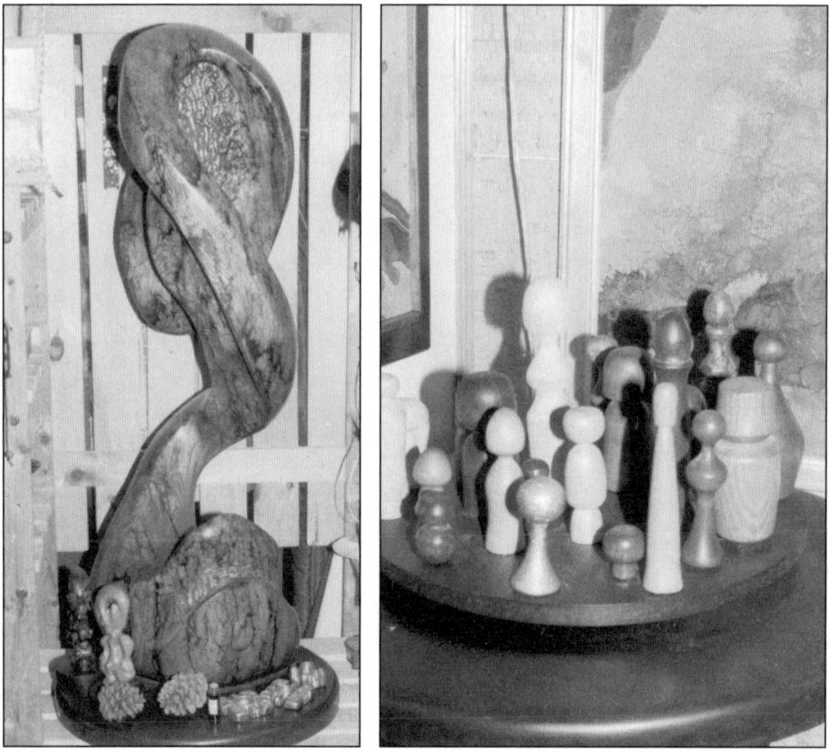

Sculptures by Tom Feenstra
From the author's collection

relocated but again was refused.[1]

He now has a studio on his property near Bancroft, Ontario, where he continues to paint and may do one sculpture a year. In the winter he lives in Toronto working at a part time job. The warmer months of the year he spends time at his country cabin and has an "open door studio week" during the summer, for visitors to peruse and purchase his creations.

---

1 *Note: The Sculputure Studio remais in its original location.*

Frances Gage
Photo from Frances Gage—Sculptor—A Retrospective
1948–1996
Publication by Art Gallery of Northumberland

A letter from Frances Gage

"My time at the Guild was brief, a week, in which I did a bas-relief of A.Y. Jackson, working with him in the little cabin at the Guild.

"Spencer and Rosa were most generous and delightful hosts, Spencer's ebullience was a wonderful foil to Rosa's shy reticence. They put both A.Y. and myself up at the Guild in what seemed great luxury.

"I executed four reliefs for Spencer Clark (now owned by the Arts and Letters Club of Toronto) namely, A.Y. Jackson, Frederick Varley, Healey Willan and Sir Ernest MacMillan. Spencer wished to do others, but they never were done.

"Spencer Clark had many programmes on "the go" aided by his seemingly boundless energy. I certainly had the impression that Rosa kept a firm rein on him. She was enormously helpful with her cultured background."

During her last year at the Ontario College of Art, Frances met the eccentric but endearing sculptors, Frances Loring and Florence Wyle. She was invited by her friend Edith Williams, a veterinarian, to dine with the two sculptors at their home and studio in an old church on Glenrose Avenue. Frances felt she was she was in the presence of two very great personalities although Frances Loring was of immense physical proportions " ... wearing elephant-sized green trousers, leaning on a cane, while her other hand was holding her old brown coat ... a tacky green beret was pulled rakishly down to one side of her head. Florence ... was dressed for the dinner outing in her old grey suit ... heavy stockings which drooped in wrinkles around her ankles.[1]" This was the beginning of 18 years of association with "the girls".

---

1 *The Girls—Rebecca Sisler—pg. 88.*

Frances Gage's sculpture reflects her classic roots and contemporary thought. Her knowledge of human anatomy is seen in her torsos and graceful figurative pieces. "...Yet there is a lean, asceticism in her work that confronts..." the attention of the viewer.

Frances Marie Gage was born in Windsor, Ontario on August 22, 1924. She later moved to Oshawa where she received her education.As a child she loved the wonders of nature and began drawing what she observed. During WWII she joined the WRENS, the women's branch of the navy. After the war she enrolled at the Ontario College of Art.

At the college she was introduced to sculpture and centred her creativity toward a profession as a sculptor. After graduation she received a small, private scholarship at the Art Students League in New York which was to last for one year. However, she lengthened her stay to two years by doing plaster casting work for more affluent students.

A few years later she was awarded a Royal Society Scholarship in Paris at the Ecole des Beaux-Arts. Living frugally she extended her stay from eight months to two years.

Back in Toronto she rented studio space from Tom Thompson at ten dollars a month. She received some commissions and also taught night school classes. Unfortunately "the shack" studio was very cold in the winter and in 1965 she acquired a small house with a backyard, on Birch Avenue.

From her backyard studio she created portraits for casting in bronze, human figure carvings, birds and beasts. "I can never portray to my satisfaction, the beauty of a creature...I can only hope to create an impression."

For one of her female torsos she was given the Rothman's Purchase Award. She was commissioned to create an enormous marble carving of "Woman" for the Women's College Hospital.

Years later she moved her studio to a country retreat north of Kitchener. Today, she works from her studio in Cobourg, Ontario overlooking Rice Lake and continues to create. "...wood is my favourite medium. It is a hard taskmaster."

Dorsey James—Sculptor

Spencer Clark tripped over "Merlin" the wooden tortoise at Gallery Danelli in Toronto, Ontario, and discovered the sculptor Dorsey James. He purchased four of his pieces of sculpture for his private collection. Years later Merlin was stolen.

Dorsey James was not aware that he had artistic talents. In Philadelphia, Pennsylvania he worked as a jet aircraft mechanic for the U.S. Air force. He had visited Canada and saw it as a beautiful country to live in.

Upon immigrating, his first job in Canada was as an assembler at DeHaviland Aircraft in Toronto. Two years later he was laid off and then employed in the office at Douglas Aircraft. Dissatisfied with this type of work, after two weeks he quit. He took a brief holiday then returned to Douglas Aircraft as a drill press operator which he soon found became a monotonous, boring job.

Depression from the repetitious job made his life miserable. His wife suggested he take a vocational test at the Y.M.C.A. Dorsey took the test and was very surprised at the results. His aptitude showed his skills were high in the arts.

Dorsey decided to go back to school and take fine arts. He was accepted at York University and the professors saw his potential. They encouraged him to try sculpting and he chose wood. A caretaker gave him advice and one day Dorsey decided to thank him by taking him a sandwich and a coffee. Under a stairway the caretaker was engaged in a discussion with someone on the facets of wood. Dorsey listened, ate the sandwich and drank the coffee. This overheard discussion cemented his desire to sculpt in wood.

Stuck in making wooden egg shapes, Dorsey finally moved beyond this stage. The sculpture was still an egg but this time with a man emerging from the inside. This sculpture was purchased by one of his professors. Dorsey said the theme of this egg is "...a universal theme. Everyone has something they're struggling to get out of."

Spencer invited Dorsey to the Guild Inn to see the sculpture cabin. Dorsey said, "...Spencer liked my work because it was alive...it had a spark of life that is so absent in so many works that you see now...the forms that I created worked so well with the material..work that had a fourth dimension of having a story behind it."

Sculptor Dorsey James
From the author's collection

Dorsey was commissioned to add Nordic sculptures to the cabin. He chose a story from Norse mythology about two warriors, Regin was the evil one, and Segurd the good. Segurd also killed the dragon Fafnir[1]. Dorsey carved Regin on the right side of the cabin doorway, in the shadows. On the left side, in the sunshine, he sculpted Segurd. Usually good should be on the right side, and evil on the left. Dorsey chose Douglas Fir, the wood of shipbuilders, for these sculptures and used a combination of urethane and lacquer thinner which penetrated into the wood and preserved it. He said, "...Spencer and I got into a little tet-a-tet over this whole thing..."

The work was almost finished when Spencer asked Dorsey to come to his office. Spencer showed him a picture of the sculpture cabin the way it used to be, gaily painted. "...You want me to put colours on those dragons...!" Spencer became angry when Dorsey disagreed.

Nevertheless, Dorsey bought the paint to apply to the dragons but couldn't do it. He was prepared to return the down-payment and leave the cabin. "...if I put on these sculptures, painted garishly...it would take away the beauty of the cabin...". Spencer came storming across the parking lot to see him, stopped, and looked at the dragons leaning against the cabin in their raw element. After a few minutes Spencer said, "Dorsey—you're right."

His work in the sculpture cabin continued for nine years. The cabin was once part of the psychiatric ward when the inn was used as a hospital. Dorsey commented , "...seems only appropriate that they'd give me the cabin that was part of the psychiatric ward...". He worked in the cabin with Tom Feenstra who lived in an apartment and had no space to work. Another sculptor was Gerd Utermann, a tall German.

---

1 *Library of the World's Mythhys & Legends—Scandinavian Mythology, H.R. Ellis Davidson, 1982 The Hamlyn Publishing Group Ltd.*

Triton Steed—Sculptor, Dorsey James
From the author's collection

Every year students from Markham District High School worked with Dorsey in the cabin, as well as other sculpture students. On several occasions he held workshops for seniors at Corycliffe.

One sculpture that he created there from cherry wood was two ravens, Odin's Huginin and Munin (thought and memory), facing in opposite directions. A lady restaurant owner was coming back to purchase this piece. Spencer Clark also wanted it. Dorsey agreed that if the lady didn't return by 5:00 p.m. that day, he would sell it to him. The lady did not come back, because of an unforseen problem, so Spencer bought the two ravens.

In the Guild's collection are several of Dorsey's sculptures. One is a snail called Chez Moi (my house) and is a different design on each side. The other is a three tailed Triton Steed made from black walnut wood.

After the Guild Inn was sold, Dorsey had a studio built onto his home. He teaches at Markham District High School and takes commissions to create sculptures. He has left a lasting memory of his years creating unique sculptures at the Guild Inn.

Aage Madsen—Sculptor

Born in Denmark, Aage Madsen spent most of his life in Canada. In 1942 he and his wife Carole had a home on an island off the coast of British Columbia. However, commissions for work in Toronto kept him in Ontario. One commission, in 1940, was for the Guild of All Arts where he designed and built the sculpture cabin.

He began as a landscape gardener with a hobby of wood carving. In Denmark his father had a handicrafts school so his son, Aage, grew up in an artistic environment. One of his brothers became an artist. Aage came to Canada in 1913 and preferred working with wood, rather than stone, marble or plaster. "Wood is a material more satisfyingly responsive."

From English oak Aage created a relief carving of Winston Churchill that skillfully caught the firmness, yet kindness, of Churchill's mouth. From Canadian copper beech he carved a buffalo which had been requested by His Royal Highness the Duke of Kent. Aage received a letter of thanks from him in August 1941.

In 1950 his sculptures were exhibited at the Art Club on Victoria Street, in Montreal, Quebec. The majority of the work was in bas- relief from birch, pine, oak and mahogany wood. Nature was the subject of his carvings. "Going North" incorporated two geese flying; "Out of the Reeds" was two black ducks taking flight. "Honey Trap" showed a bear pawing the earth to get at a bees' nest. Natives interested Aage and he depicted an Eskimo woman in a parka, with a child, looking over her shoulder, which was described as "...a truly engaging work of sympathy and understanding." (*The Gazette, Montreal, P.Q. Apr. 8, 1950)*

An article in the *Toronto Daily Star*, April 8, 1950 says about his sculpture, "...the geese and the sweep of wide wings give...a powerful rhythm...the way he uses the character of the wood rather than attempt to disguise it..."

Nicapetre (Peter Balanca)—Sculptor 1936

Born in Bralitza, Romania in 1936, Nicapetre lived under the communist regime and after fifteen years finally gained a passport enabling him to travel to a symposium in Greece. His abstract designs were considered decadent art by the oppressive regime and he wanted more freedom to create. After the symposium he defected and a year later was accepted as a refugee to Canada. In 1991 he displayed several pieces at the Guild Inn through Scarborough Arts Council's "Temporary Contemporary Show."

Large sculpture needs large spaces to be created, so Nicapetre was given permission to work on the grounds of the Guild Inn, "...hidden behind bushes near the ravine where the caretakers put things they cut down from the park." He worked there for three years and visitors enjoyed seeing him create. Unfortunately, he had to take his tools back and forth each time. Then in 1992 he requested the use of the Duncan barn on the Guild property. Bureaucracy was dismayed and distressed that a sculptor with all his mess and noise, was working at the Guild Inn.

Chairman of the Board of Management, Bernard Rasch, had this to say. "...The position of the Board of Management is that no artist can claim squatters rights on the park property, because the danger is, that if you let one come in, how can you stop others from coming in? And then you could end up with an unregulated artists' colony in an unregulated, unauthorized fashion."[1] Nicapetre was forced off the property.

"...During my 11 years spent in Canada I earned my living doing various types of work but never abandoned the art of drawing and sculpture. I consider that my art has gained in profundity and mastery in Canada, due to the climate of spiritual freedom in which we live."

---

1 *Eye, October 28, 1993—Malene Arpe*

Sculptor Nicapetre
From author's collection

As a child Nicapetre loved to draw, supported in this endeavour by his carpenter father. At age 16 his father died and he was forced to abandon his studies and work to support his mother and five sisters. For four years he worked as a labourer but kept up his painting. Then he met a stage designer who liked his work and offered him a better job.

For three years he worked for a puppet theatre company modeling faces and making costumes. At this time there was a need for soldiers. However, as head of his family he could postpone his military service. Then he took an examination to complete his schooling and was accepted at the Academy of Arts in Bucharest.

After six years of study he became a high school teacher, teaching drawing and art history as well as sculpting in his studio. His work was highly recognized and for ten years he worked as a full-time sculptor. When he defected he told no one of his plans not knowing who to trust. He left all his work and his studio. Friends secretly removed his sculptures before his studio was destroyed. In 1989, when the Communist regime was overthrown, he was able to visit his homeland.

Nicapetre was pleased to see that some of his work had survived. Most of the work he created in Romania is now owned by the Bucharest Museum.

His sculptures are in many countries of the world, and he won the International Competition in Japan. To commemorate the ten years after the death of Glenn Gould, he created "Cadences for Glenn" which was on display at the Royal Conservatory of Music. These three pieces are still owned by him. Marble, stone and wood are the materials he likes to use, such as maple wood, poplar, ash and oak.

After a tornado tore through the town of Kirkfield, Ontario, a lot of trees were felled at the McKenzie Inn. The owner decided to have the trees carved rather than removed. Nicapetre was one of the sculptors chosen and from a fallen fir tree he created a unique design called a "Pod" that was open and releasing seeds. The sculpture which took him three weeks to complete, is still on that property.

After his expulsion from the Guild Inn property, Nicapetre needed a new studio. Alexandra Siemanuk of Scarborough's municipal office, was asked to help him locate new space to work in.

Sculptor Nicapetre
From the author's collection

She spoke to Helen Campbell, widow of Scarborough's former mayor Albert Campbell, and she was delighted to offer him the use of her barn. He works there during the summer as the barn is too cold during the winter months. In winter he paints and has written a book in his native language about the history of education and art during the Communist regime.

Virgil Untila describes his work as: "Nicapetre's sculptures replace nothing...instead they are expressions of his ability to perceive the presence of the gods, of his need for higher beings, and his quest to retrace their existence...the space lodging Nicapetre's works is thereby transformed...with its own co-ordinates, featuring...points where angles of shadow and darkness dance with wide and luminous forms."

Sculptor Siggy Puchta
From the author's collection

Sculptor—Siggy Puchta 1933

In 1969 a gallery went bankrupt and Siggy Puchta's show was cancelled. Rosa and Spencer's daughter Ruth, heard of the cancellation and the show was moved to the Guild Inn. While visitors viewed his large creations he sat in the Sculpture Cabin and created miniatures of animals. Visitors bought these tiny bronzed figures, ranging in height from 3 to 5 inches. While there, he also created chess pieces.

These chess pieces were not the familiar kings, pawns, knights and queens. Instead he made 5" high figures of North American Indians. He creates the forms with modeling wax. At the foundry they are covered with a porcelain-like material and placed in an oven. The wax melts and the cavity is filled with bronze. This becomes an "original" and after being smoothed and unwanted blemishes removed, molds are constructed. The miniatures are then made from the molds as often as required.

"...As a kid I was always playing with plasticine...making little men...my father was a woodcarver...in those days you followed...I didn't really want to...I was more into drawing...".

Siggy still plays with plasticine. A life-sized figure in his garage studio is made with plasticine and its shape was being changed to create a new figure.

Siegfried (Siggy) Puchta was born in 1933 in Griez, Germany. His childhood was spent in the town of Zulenroda, and at age four he showed great interest in drawing and modeling with plasticine. After one year at high school he returned to public school to learn the trade of woodcarver. In April 1951 his love of freedom was threatened and he fled East Germany to the small town of Bad Münder. For two years he worked as a woodcarver and was able to bicycle to Italy, Austria and Switzerland to study the work of the old masters. This created an overwhelming desire to create his own work. In 1953, at the age of nineteen, his application for immigration to Canada was approved, and with the consent of his parents, he moved to Malton, Ontario.

A child's head by sculptor Siggy Puchta
From the author's collection

Three bears—sculpture at the Toronto Zoo
From the author's collection

Sculptor Siggy Puchta in his workshop
From the author's collection

He became a farmhand but kept up his carving and modeling. This led to a job as a woodcarver in the art furniture department of Ridpath's. After a year, still keeping his job at Ridpath's, he was employed as a stone carver in a monument shop. At night-school classes at Humber Valley, in 1957, he began teaching woodcarving. Then in 1958, at the age of twenty-five, Siggy became a Canadian citizen.

While sitting on a beach, vacationing in Acapulco, Siggy watched the passing vendors and they became models for the figures of his Aztecs chess set. Most often he uses pictures rather than models, and watches movies for the movements of people, such as dancers and athletes. He has a great interest in sports, reflected in his creation of football player figures, ballet dancers, skiers and skaters and is an accomplished water skier.

Creating models in wax is more effective than from a one-sided drawing. "...work in three dimensional...when you make a drawing you can't go behind it...then I carve it whatever size in stone or wood...".

In a basement workshop he creates miniatures. For stone sculptures, some eight feet high, he works in the facilities of a monument company and uses their equipment. In limestone he creates religious figures, one was of St. Luke, another the virgin Mary. These religious figures are purchased by churches and cemeteries as well as smaller ones for headstones.

With large bronze figures, they have to be hollow inside. "...when you get up to a certain size you have to make them hollow...". At the foundry an inside cavity is created and the bronze poured in between. Then the pieces are welded together. A fish sculpture mold was created with sand, aluminum was then pressed into wet sand at the foundry and a pattern made. Bronze is then poured into this mold and the pieces welded together. This particular piece was sold to a private individual in Nassau.

Throughout Canada and the United States, his creations are on display. In 1965, after the first outdoor sculpture show at the Stratford Shakespearian Festival, he was accepted as a member of the Sculptors Society of Canada.

The variety of his sculptures reach many places. He has designed and created awards for long-time employees of Consumer's

Gas, an old gas lamplighter lighting a lamp. He has created medallions for the Marshall McLuhan Award, for the Canadian Nuclear Association and the Fred Gardiner Award, just to mention a few. He has also created bronze horses for the Jockey Club of Canada. One 12" bronze figure was of a Bunny Girl. Hugh Hefner wanted it but wouldn't pay more than $25.00 for it, which was far less than the cost to produce. It was sold to someone else.

Harry Oakes Jr., son of the infamous Oakes murdered in the Bahamas, ordered a 6' Dolphin. The sculpture weighed almost two tons. While it was being lifted into a truck for shipping, it almost became a disaster. A rope on the lifting crane suddenly began splitting but fortunately the operator brought the sculpture down before it smashed into pieces.

His work is sold through galleries and by his reputation and is found in many locations. In Sarnia at a border crossing, visitors are welcomed by his Canadian Geese with a seven foot wing span. At the Metro Toronto Zoo children love his mother bear and two cubs. He commented about his sculpture of a heron with a fish in its mouth, "...water spits out of the fish's mouth...I've never seen a heron spit water..or a frog...".

Arthur John Tracey—Sculptor 1910

In 1924, at the age of 14, Arthur Tracey came to Canada from Middlesex, England, to study at the Ontario College of Art. He worked as a farm labourer in Port Hope, Ontario and in 1929 studied sculpting at night school under sculptor Emmanuel Hahn. He won several scholarships and worked in clay and plaster. In 1931 he became an assistant instructor at the OCA.

Arthur had a studio in Chelsea, England until 1938 when he joined the R.A.F. (Royal Air Force) as World War II began. He was transferred in 1944 to the Royal Canadian Air Force. After the war, in 1947, he again became an instructor at the Ontario College of Art. He later became an Art Master at the Shawinigan Lake School in British Columbia and also worked in California.

On October 8, 1949, the Globe and Mail newspaper recorded his thoughts on the attitude of Californians to artists and of Canadians.

> *"The basic difference seems to me that in California, the artist and the designer are really regarded as professionals, while in Canada the artist is treated as a kind of amateur."*

He is listed as working as a sculptor at the Guild Inn at some point in time. Several of his works were displayed at the Canadian National Exhibition and in 1947 he displayed a terra cotta torso. In May 1948 the Toronto Star had a photo of a terra cotta bust of Joan Michener. The caption stated, "An air of classical serenity has been achieved by the simple disposition of the masses and through the gently flowing lines which surround the focal element of the face." In 1962 he was living in North Vancouver.

Sculptor Gerd Untermann at work in his studio
From the author's collection

Gerd Hanns Oscar Untermann—Sculptor 1930

"...divine madness...forces me to give touchable shape to images that come unbidden and unexpected...To be subjected to this psychic and physical demand on one's energy and resources leads to a double life...My justification for leading that kind of life in an environment that puts great emphasis on the tangible assets, is my work...that I carry on a family tradition that surfaced first with the sculptor Slvter who enhanced the Cathedral of Rheims in the 14th Century."

Gerd Untermann was born in 1930 in Brun, Germany, during the Nazi era. He couldn't understand the "exclusiveness" turmoil. It didn't make sense to him. He said, "There has to be more to life than accumulating things that can so easily be destroyed." So he pursued the intangible through his art.

In 1949 he became a tradesman making fine furniture. In 1953 he emigrated to Canada, built houses in Kenora, Ontario, and became a Canadian citizen in 1958. Then he decided to pursue another career.

Gerd studied to become a United Church minister. However, once again, he didn't fit in this society. He saw the church dogma as another form of "exclusiveness", and questioned other religious faiths wondering why each was segmented from the other. He felt that each religion was similar although expressed in different ways. Gerd left and tried another profession.

Without a BA (Bachelor of Arts) he was accepted into the law firm of Mendelson and Beatty. He articled for 1 1/2 years running errands and handling small cases. Then he decided he didn't want to "...be for sale as a lawyer." In cases of poor people who had been ripped off by various companies, he tried to help them avoid these pitfalls rather than prosecute them.

His art skill was still a large part of his life. Gerd created a 2' sculpture of a girl carrying a Greek vase and then put it in a store for sale. It sold twenty minutes later and the store owner asked him to do two more. He decided to pursue a career as a sculptor and went to the

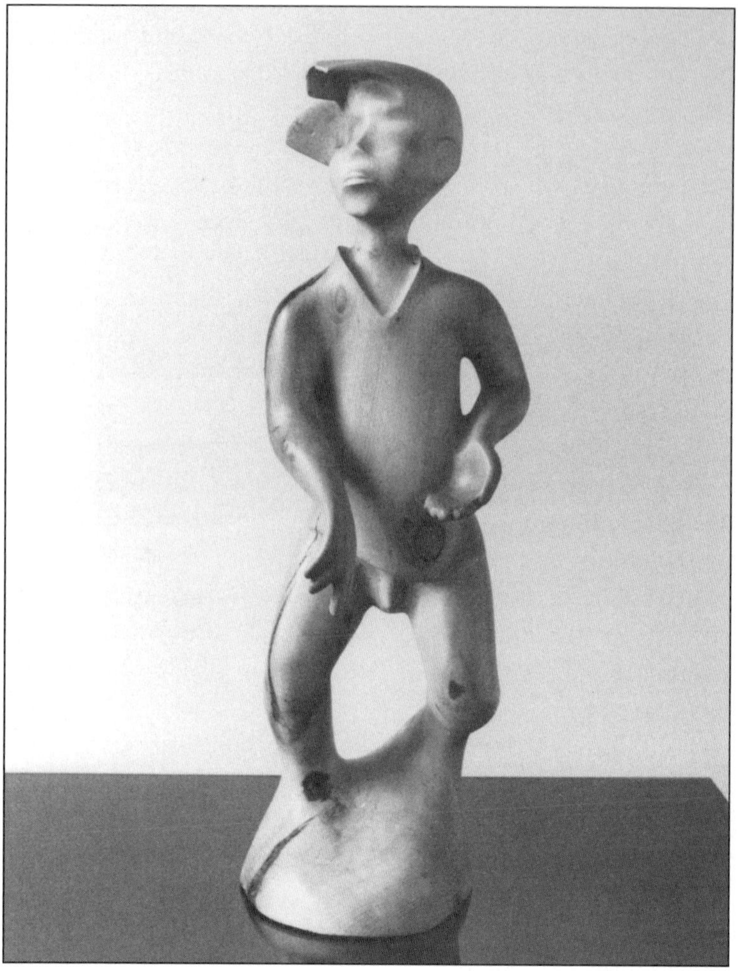

Sculpture by Gerd Untermann
From the collection of The Guild

Ontario College of Art.

A professor at the college asked him what he was doing there. Gerd told him about his sculptures and that he was already selling his creations. The professor told him that he didn't need to study at the college to shape his art style.

To make money so he could work on his sculptures, Gerd returned to his skills as a carpenter. He worked on one house for 3 1/2 years creating a Hungarian-style kitchen. The kitchen cabinets are pine, including handles shaped like tulips, butterflies and apples. The inlaid floor design of the house was done with 10,000 hand cut pieces.

After many shows of his work at various galleries from 1964 until 1977, he tired of the routine and in 1980 met the man who became a work partner and inspiration.

He met Dorsey James and the two of them worked harmoniously together in the Sculpture Cabin at the Guild Inn. Often they adjourned to the Guild's pub enjoying the music of the piano player, singing, meeting other patrons then returned to the cabin to work. They fired each other's imagination and often worked into the early hours of the morning without feeling tired. Gerd found the atmosphere at the Guild Inn very inspiring. But he doesn't remember ever meeting Spencer Clark.

One time while working on a sculpture of his girl friend, Gerd didn't know how to position her arms. In a dream the answer came. He positioned the arms comfortably across her stomach. Sculpture designs occur to him in other ways.

Gerd said, "Art gives warmth and hope...art should not increase misery...take conflicting phenomena and create harmony...artists can make peace."

He was approached to do a sculpture of a woman. He talked to her by telephone and the image design appeared in his mind. The sculpture of the woman showed only half of her, the rest hidden. She was so surprised to see that he had captured her personality so well, in that she only showed part of her feelings to people.

Another time, Gerd was approached by a man named George, who wanted a sculpture of his wife. The difficulty was that the wife had died. In thinking of this image he was overcome by a feeling that he was George and saw what the wife looked like. After the sculpture

Sculpture of a woman by Gerd Untermann
From the collection of The Guild

was created, George didn't want to see it. This sculpture was then put into a show and George hung around the gallery to see it. He was so upset at the likeness to his wife, he went to a bar and got drunk.

Gerd's friend, whose daughter had died of a brain tumour, had a vision. He'd seen his daughter with Christ behind her. The man wanted him to create a statue of this vision. In a week and he created a sketch which was exactly what the man had seen. He made the sketch into a stone statue and with special permission it was erected in the Elgin Mills Cemetery as the family's headstone.

Dorsey James was too busy to do a statue using the thin stump of an ash tree. He gave this commission to Gerd who corresponded with the lady whose husband, Peter, had died. He'd married the widow with four children and became a wonderful husband and father. The sculpture was created within two weeks. He says most of his work usually takes years to complete.

The statue is almost 7' tall of Peter holding onto a bird while a young child leans against him. The statue looks exactly like Peter and his eyes seem to follow the viewer around. As this statue is still a living tree, preservatives must be poured inside the head everyday. If this is not done, the trunk would crack. The owner herself applies the preservative.

Today Gerd lives and works in a studio in Claremont, on a piece of property designated for an airport. The area inspires his creativity and he happily pursues his career as a sculptor. However, he fondly remembers his time at the Guild Inn working in the sculpture cabin with "Slim".

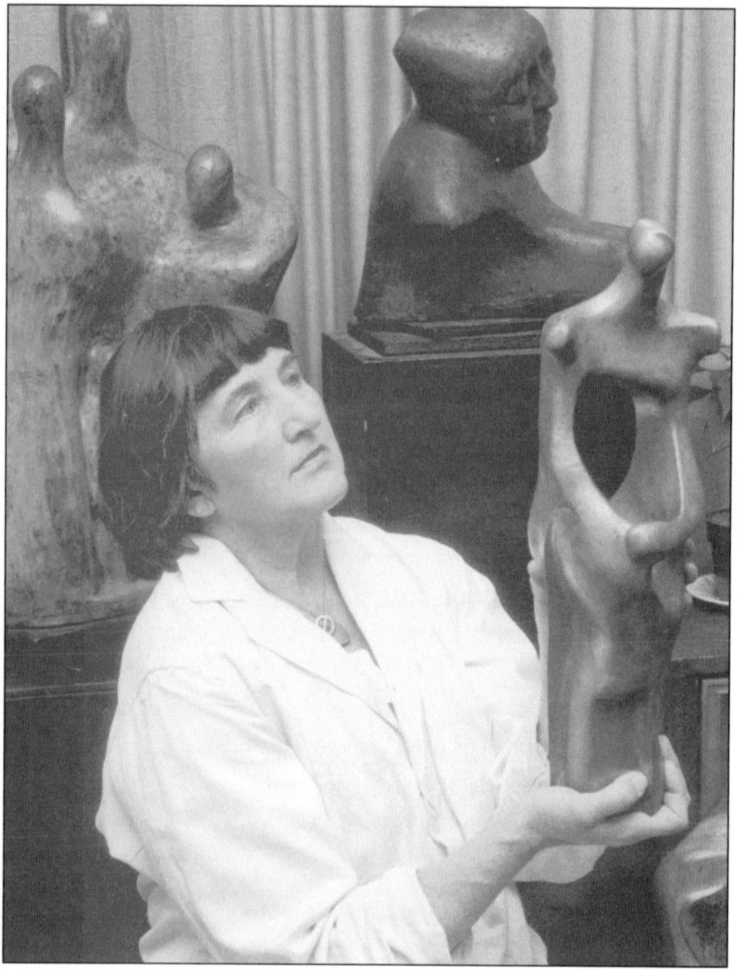

Sculptor Elizabeth Fraser Williamson—April 1978
From the collection of The Guild
Copyright of The Toronto Star Syndicate—used with permission

Sculptor—Elizabeth Fraser Williamson 1914–2000

Once upon a time, beside a cabin in the woods, stood the head of a sacred bull with long graceful horns. Staring eyes peered down from round faces hanging on the tall tree trunks. Grouped figures stretched toward each other in what seemed to be a joyous dance. A hushed atmosphere greeted the interloper pausing to enjoy escape from a busy world into one of beauty and wonder. In the cabin the creator created. — *Carole M. Lidgold*

Elizabeth Fraser Williamson discovered her talent for sculpture with a 5 lb. package of Reeve's Permanent clay to make jewellery. She was not interested in making jewellery. "...I'm interested in the human face and how it changes from different races...maybe I'll make a series of brooches with faces...".

At that time she had three young children, farm animals to care for and a large garden. After creating the faces, one a full face, a three-quarter face and a profile, she discovered she wasn't excited about her creations. "...If I'm not excited I'm on the wrong track...it was too restrictive...".

Elizabeth was born in 1914 in Vancouver, British Columbia and grew up in Ottawa, Ontario. At 12 years old she was the youngest student enrolled in the Fine Arts College, where four years later, she graduated with honours. In 1970 Spencer Clark invited her to become the sculptor-in-residence and live in a cabin at the Guild Inn. She taught sculpting to students in the Osterhaut Cabin, for 23 years. In the cottage where she lived she sculpted with clay, unfired, because firing changes the look of the sculpture. "...I want it (the sculpture) just as it comes from my hand...". Not firing the pieces makes them fragile. Sometimes bronze casts are made of the sculptures and limited edition copies are made.

The clay sculptures are dried slowly. "...you put saran wrap over it and make a little tent so that the air in there stays constant...then I put wax on it just to keep the dust off and seal it in a little more...and sometimes I paint them...with acrylic paint...".

"...I really love experimenting, I love the excitement of taking chances...if things go wrong and it becomes a wreck, I'm not too disturbed because my philosophy is it's how you as a person and an artist develop that is important...".

A double sided, two face sculpture, entitled *Shoona's Dream* tells the story of an adopted child. An Inuit mother loves the child who feels the loss of her own people. Shoona, the child, has a dream about the Great Spirit who transports her to a lake. Here a ghostly presence touches her, strokes her hair and Shoona finally feels accepted by her adopted family. There is a story about each of Elizabeth's pieces.

In 1983 Penumbra Press, Vancouver, published a book with photographs of Elizabeth's sculptures with her poetry and stories. On page 40 is the story of the Sacred Bull and a photograph of the head.

> *"As soon as the Sacred Bull was born I knew the clue to his right place lay in the curve of his horns. That great sweeping arc must frame something significant."*

In 1995 Elizabeth was forced to move from the cabin. Her entire sculpture collection of 175 pieces was purchased by the Joseph and Wolf LeBovic Foundation and housed in the LeBovic Gallery in Scarborough.[1] However she did not move far from the Guild Inn. The cabin where she lived has been demolished as well as other cabins on the Guild Inn property.

Note: Elizabeth Fraser Williamson died on February 23, 2000 at age 86. Elizabeth lived in Guildwood Villa Nursing Home, a short walk from the Guild Inn.

---

1 *The Lebovic Gallery closed in 1999.*

Woodworking

Algot Clarence Nelson—Woodworking 1915–1993

Woodworker Clarence Nelson was born in November 1915 in a one car garage. The garage was located on 160 acres of land, 40 miles north-east of Lethbridge, Alberta, in a town called Enchant. His Swedish parents lived in the garage with two other sons, until they had enough money to build a house. The material for the house, costing $1,000.00, came from Eaton's store. The basement was dug by hand. There was no hydro in the house and had a "privy" out back. On the prairies winter temperatures were often 54 degrees below zero. Clarence lived here until he was nine years old.

The family moved to another farm with better irrigation, but once again suffered crop failures. Near Lethbridge, Alberta, the land provided good crops but with an infestation of rattle snakes. The family moved again to a rented farm in Vulcan, Alberta, a good crop area. At the Thigh Public School Clarence created his first piece of woodwork, a corner bracket using a hand-held fretsaw. Then he made a treadle jig saw at home from a picture he saw in Hobby's Limited Catalogue, and began woodworking. He made an inlaid picture and a story about him was printed in a local paper. In 1939, while living in Ensign, Alberta, he saw an article in the Calgary Herald about the Guild of All Arts. He wrote to Rosa and Spencer telling them about the work he was doing in marquetry (inlaid wood pieces formed into pictures or different patterns). They responded with a letter requesting a photograph of his work. He sent them a picture of one of his creations, an elk in a mountain scene, and he was invited to become one of the craftsmen at the Guild of All Arts. Clarence's train fare was paid by the Guild and he was offered a small allowance of $1.00 per week, in addition to room and board.

Clarence had arrived at Union Station and took a Gray Coach bus to Scarborough. He missed the stop for the Guild and ended up almost in Pickering. However, he finally arrived at his destination and began an apprenticeship with a cabinet maker. The log cabin became his home and he created pictures which were sold in the gift shop. A short while later he was offered a job at the sum of $1.00 per hour, and he left the Guild.

At the beginning of World War II he worked as an assistant foreman at Massey Harris' mosquito bomber wing assembly plant in Woodstock, Ontario. Massey Harris provided accommodation and meals when Clarence married his wife Dolly. He was soon moved back to Toronto where they lived in Weston, Ontario.

Children were not welcome in a rented house so he and his wife were forced to move after the birth of their first daughter. On University Avenue, on the former Mary Pickford estate, he purchased a small trailer where he and his family lived for six years. During that time he spent 18 months in the armed service. After the war a unique opportunity was offered. Would he rebuild a burned out trailer on its original chassis? He was also asked to build new trailers. Then he decided to form his own company, Nelson Trailers, and began building them for himself to sell.

Moving his family to Lloydtown, Ontario, Clarence built trailers for two dealers in Toronto and several trailers for Dr. Ballard's Dog Food. These were mobile zoos that travelled around Ontario.

In 1957 the Canadian Mobile Home Show was held at the Guild of All Arts. Clarence returned to the Guild but only to take photographs for his scrapbook.

In London, Ontario, in 1965, he accepted his first steady job. He worked at the General Motors Diesel plant where he was employed for fifteen years. He retired from there when he was 65 years old. Dolly had terminal cancer and died in 1980.

Clarence had purchased an old house in London, Ontario, that had been condemned by the health department because the plumbing froze in the winter. The plumbing was repaired and the house became his next home. Here he built trailers on consignment for individual people. He built his last mini motor home on a new 1983 Ford pickup truck. The body and interior were built in separate pieces in the basement of his house and assembled on the truck in the spring. This was built so he and his grandson could travel together. Then his grandson joined the Air Force. Clarence sold his home and moved into Chelsey Park, a nursing home where he made wooden crafts for the activity groups, people with arthritis to finish.

Clarence died on September 15, 1993 in London, Ontario.

Herman Riedl—Master Cabinet Maker 1894–1972

Rosa Clark purchased raspberries from a farmer's wife on Scarborough Golf Club Road. The farmer was a master cabinet maker named Herman Riedl. Spencer Clark liked his work and Herman became part of the Guild of All Arts for thirty-two years.

Herman Riedl was born in 1894 in Bavaria, Germany. He apprenticed as a cabinet maker and took the master's exam. In 1924 he left behind his wife, Anna, and went to Canada. A year later he brought Anna to Canada where they first lived on Pape Avenue in Toronto. Later they bought three acres in Scarborough, the Danielle farm, on Scarborough Golf Club Road. They had one daughter, Anne, who still lives in the area of Guildwood Village. The red brick house that Herman built still stands on the corner of Dunelm and Scarborough Golf Club Road.

The cabinet shop was in the Studio until 1953. He made looms, which were sold to the public, the speed loom being the best seller. Rosa often bought antiques that needed restoration. Herman, a perfectionist in his work, restored these pieces to their original beauty.

Some of the vanities in the guest rooms were constructed by him. He often had assistants, one of them Frank Mildred. They worked together for two years, then Frank returned to England.

In the late 1940s Spencer purchased property known as Crestwood Golf Course. A two storey club house on the property, which was once owned by Levi Annis, became the woodworking shop. Herman worked from this location, which was closer to his home than the Studio, until 1965 when he retired at age 71.

Herman also helped in the creation of educational toys. In 1941 these toys were made under the label of Guildcraft Educational Playthings. For children 3 to 7 years of age there was a wooden liner and freighter, boats for water fun, priced at $3.50 for the set. Other water toys included tugs, barges, a ferry, lighthouse and a buoy. There were wheel trains, a toddler's floor train, priced up to $6.50. Peg boards were for senior children or juniors, and a puzzle box wagon for toddlers. A Humpty Dumpty piler was a series of disks to put on a standup base. A pep peg pounder for $3.00 was a "captivating" toy for young children to develop muscles and co-ordination. There were blocks, beads and wooden puzzles in shapes of animals, ducks and boats.

Herman Riedl died in October 1972 at the age of 78. He loved working with wood and as a perfectionist, was always proud of the items he created and restored. The house he built is a testament to the work he loved.

Artists

A.J. Casson with Lorraine Thomson
Taken from movie "The Guild Inn"
From the collection of The Guild

Alfred Joseph Casson—Artist 1898–1992

Rosa's cousin, A. Y. Jackson, was a member of the famed Canadian artists known as the "Group of Seven". Another of these members was artist Alfred Casson who did sketches in water colour and oil paint. His landscapes were of areas such as the Muskokas, Haliburton and Lake Superior.

Alfred Casson was born in Toronto, and at age nine his family moved to Guelph, Ontario. Here he roamed the countryside which inaugurated his love of nature. When the family moved to Hamilton, Ontario, he studied at the Technical School. At age 16 he became an apprentice.

He was employed at Laidlaw Lithography and retouched photos and engraved on zinc plates. The cramped facilities were filthy and the air was saturated with heavy chemical odours which he detested. Alfred worked at many printing companies and became experienced in all aspects of this field.

Painting was just a hobby and he took night school classes at the Ontario College of Art. Some of his relatives lived in Meadowvale, a small town on the Credit River, where he painted the local scenery. On other sketching excursions with the art class he painted Ontario's scenery.

His employment at Rous and Mann, a printing company, changed his life and led him to a man who helped increase his artistic skills. As an apprentice to the senior designer, Franklin Carmichael, he found a friend and tutor. Franklin was later instrumental in creating the "Group of Seven."

Other employees at Rous and Mann painted in their free time. Alfred organized a group called the "Palette Workers Club." Franklin was impressed with Alfred's paintings and invited him to join the Arts and Letters Club of Toronto. Club members comprised of writers, artists, musicians, actors and benefactors. Alfred often travelled with the Group of Seven on painting excursions to areas such as the Muskokas.

In 1920 Alfred had his first solo show at the Arts and Letters Club. He sold his first painting in 1921 after its acceptance in the annual exhibition of the Ontario Society of Artists. The Group of

Seven often invited him to exhibit his work with them, and instead of being asked to join the group after one of the members left, was told by Franklin Carmichael that he had been automatically accepted into the group. In 1932, the Group of Seven artists disbanded.

In 1924 he married Margaret Petry, and two years later was employed by Sampson-Matthews a creative design house. He worked here until his retirement in 1958, when he left to pursue painting on a full-time basis.

In 1954 he received a gold medal for his distinguished service in advertising and the Order of Canada in 1991.

Some of Alfred's artistic endeavours boosted the moral of overseas military personnel. He lobbied the government and they finally agreed to hang copies of Canadian paintings in messes, canteens and offices. He insisted that the government establish a war artists programme and was appointed to the Canadian War Artists Committee. In 1980 when a promotional film was made of the Guild Inn, Alfred Casson was interviewed by Lorraine Thomson.

A change occurred to his painting style in the 1950s. Previously he had done colourful nature scenes. He began to paint scenes exploring the atmospheric and dramatic lighting effects of thunderstorms and rain storms, which created a mystical feeling. This style continued until the late 1960s when he returned to painting a "less stylized scheme."

In 1992, at age 94, Alfred Casson died and is buried in Kleinburg, at the McMichael Canadian Art Collection, in a cemetery for the Group of Seven artists.

Rody Kenny Courtice—Artist 1895–1973

In 1998 Alicia Boutilier wrote a book entitled "*4 Women Who Painted in the 1930s and 1940s*". One of these women, Rody Kenny Courtice was connected to the Guild of All Arts. She once owned Corycliff where she painted landscapes in the style of the Group of Seven. Born in Renfrew, Ontario, Rody studied at the Ontario College of Arts. As well as painting, she had studied the art of puppetry and stage craft at Hart House Theatre and in Chicago. She became a children's art instructor at the Art Gallery. However, with 13 year old students on Saturday morning she found them to be lethargic and hard to get them to work on paintings.

Rody used a unique method to motivate the young students. She had a whistle and blew it in class to startle them into paying attention. After the shrill blast, the students began learning the art of painting.

Art could be created in other ways and Rody taught this to students and teachers. Using discarded material such as paper, pulp and local clay, she taught them how to create art and recycle discards into an art form.

Sketching took Rody and her friends to the remote areas of northern Ontario. They travelled to mining towns such as Cobalt and Kirkland Lake to sketch their landscapes. Her mine paintings invoked romantic desolation with darkened windows and an absence of people. In 1947 in the annual report of the Canadian Group of Painters her painting "Mines, Northern Ontario" was described as the subject being dominated by machinery.

Rody's paintings sometimes poked fun at the Group of Seven artists. A Tom Thomson painting shows a twisted pine on a barren landscape. She painted a humble sumach tree on a barren prominence. Some later paintings, when she began expressing her own creativity rather than follow the Group of Seven style, were abstract. In her "Grandiflora Bianca" the flowers are outlined, bordered by blue and green leaves on a background of impressionistic brush strokes.

At one time, she took a six month hiking tour of Europe to visit galleries and observe at art schools. Her paintings were often exhibited at the Royal Canadian Academy. In 1931 she was one of 26 Canadian artists to design a Christmas card for the "Painters of Canada". The design was of her sister at play. To represent women's war work in World War I, she designed a poster called "Nurses are Needed", which won second prize in the Art Gallery of Toronto's poster contest. In 1923 she became an assistant librarian at the Ontario College of Art a position which she held until 1927.

Rody's work often designated her as a humorous painter. This seemed to jeopardize her being considered as a serious artist. Her painting "Pet Rooster" reveals her candor and joy of life, her humour and whims. The author of "*4 Women Who Painted...*" suggests that Rody is the least recognized of the four women artists.

The Arts and Letters Club of Toronto was important to artists but it was for "men only". In 1909 the Heliconian Club was formed by professional women from music, writing, painting and drama. In 1932-33 Rody became the president. The artist section was responsible for decorating the facilities at 35 Hazelton Avenue which was the Carpenter's Gothic church, for their annual Christmas party. In 1944 the party was on a Greek theme. Rody and her friends did murals in black and white terra cotta as their interpretation of Greek mythology.

Women's paintings were not discriminated against by the public, critics or juries. In a 1948 article in Chatelaine Magazine, women artists stated that they couldn't make a living by painting pictures—they had to do commercial work as well. Painting was not a hobby—it was hard work!

Rody's first husband was killed in WWI. She remarried, to Roy Courtice a lawyer, and they had a son, Paul. Several of her paintings are in the collection of the Guild Inn and were recently on display.

Joachim Gauthier—Painting and Drawing 1897

Joachim Gauthier was born in 1897 at North Bay, Ontario. He studied art at Tacoma, Washington and was a commercial artist for 37 years at Sampson-Matthews. He painted realistic landscapes and impressionistic images using oil and watercolours. He is listed in The Guild files as one of the artists that worked there.

Artist—Nicholas Hornyanski
From the collection of The Guild

Nicholas Hornyanski—Artist

During the summer of 1935 Nicholas Hornyanski held an art course at the Guild Inn. This was the same summer when silversmith Arthur Kirk gave lessons on his craft. At other times, students from the Beaux Arts Ateliers, a school operated by Nicholas, took sketching trips to the Guild Inn.

Instruction in these classes included learning how to draw and paint the human form. Drawings were done in pencil, charcoal, pen and ink sketches, water colours, tempera and oil paint. The three month term cost $60.00 and could be either morning, afternoon or evening classes.

Apprentices were given the opportunity to observe his methods in batik, metal work and transfer methods. One of his sketches of Corycliff Lodge was used on the front of note cards and sold in the Guild Inn's gift shop.

Artists Colonel Edward Thomson and his daughter Gaille
From the collection of The Guild

Colonel Edward L. Thomson—Painter and Sculptor 1879–1960

Edward Thomson was born in Aldershot, England and educated for army service. His military career took him to France and major battles of WWI. He received the Distinguished Service Order presented personally by King George. In 1921 he brought his family to Canada and was employed with the Ontario Hydro Commission.

He and his wife had four children, a boy and three girls. He encouraged them to have hobbies and to draw what they saw and felt. His own paintings were mystical and depicted, in a symbolic way, the adventures of the human soul. In their teens the four children formed an amazing group of creative artists. They had their work accepted and published by newspaper and magazines. At age 14, his son Cecil, won a monetary prize for his caricatures of film celebrities. One daughter, Gaille, painted with her father at the Guild Inn.

Edward was also an illustrator. For the MacMillan publishing company he illustrated "Aesop's Fables" and designed jacket covers for their other books. Sculpting was another talent he used to create art and did a bust of Voltaire. As well, he was an expert weaver which he emphasized was not only for women. Writing was another skill he used in articles for "The Canadian Theosophist Magazine." He was also the editor of the "Legion News."

In Toronto Edward Thomson founded two arts clubs—the Amateur Art Club and the Arts Club. As a writer, he was a member of the Canadian Authors Association. He was also General Secretary of the Theosophical Society in Canada whose belief about God and the world was based on mystical insight.

A serious heart condition caused his death on November 14, 1960. In a tribute from Dr. Henry A. Smith, his eulogy stated, "...I became aware of the geniability and warmth of his personality and of his fine sense of humour." From Cedric Weaver, "...I have known him as a gentle man, an artist of many talents—printing, sculpturing and fine draughtsmanship..."

Music, Theatre and Photography

Musicians Jan, Mark and Boris Hamburg
From the collection of The Guild

Music, Theatre and Photography

Music

Cecil Barnum-Kappey

For three years Cecil Barum-Kappey played dinner music on the grand piano in the front hall. He smoked cigarettes using a long holder and dressed elegantly. An excellent pianist, he played classical music, songs from Broadway shows and music he had written. He lived on Kingston Road in an old stone, coach house with his wife and two daughters. At one time he had been part of a band that performed at the Banff Springs Hotel, at Lake Louise in Alberta, during the 1920s.

Boris Berlin

- He gave music lessons at the Guild Inn for students attending the Guildwood's School.

Virginia Knott

- (see letter excerpt) She rented Corycliff, three bedrooms, and a kitchen for $350.00 per month. There was space for 24 students but she started with 12.

The Hamburg Brothers

- worked with Boris Berlin and spent a month at the Guild Inn rehearsing for a concert tour.

Sir Ernest MacMillan

He spent one summer at the Guild Inn composing new music while relaxing beneath the trees.

Musician Sir Ernest MacMillan
From the collection of The Guild

Theatre

There were several drama groups which produced outdoor plays such as "Midsummer Night's Dream" and "Dear Brutus". A Shakespearean Festival was held at Trinity College by the Earle Grey Players, and some of their plays were held outdoors at the Guild Inn. However, plans to construct an outdoor amphitheatre with stone from the Stanley Barracks, was put in abeyance as the theatre at Stratford, Ontario became a huge success.

Photography

A lecture was held at the Guild Inn by Mr. Jaycocks who brought the miniature Leica camera to Canada. His lecture was on the use of miniature cameras for candid photography. The Guild Inn had its own photographic laboratory which was the responsibility of Frank Pogue and Orville Allen.

Virginia Knott—Musician

The following is an excerpt from an article she wrote for Rosa Clark's 90th birthday party held on January 19, 1978.

"More than 40 years ago I first came out to The Guild of All Arts to find a "Little Haven" from a busy schedule on the Faculty of The Royal Conservatory of Music. It was a truly wonderful spot to:

1. Have breakfast in bed, ordered the night before
2. In those days picking a few of the profusion of wild flowers
3. Count on being wakened by the steam radiators creaking in the night!

"Edna and Paul Breithaupt were treasured friends of mine and there were lovely parties at New Years. One I remember a few years later when sculptor Peter Hills came for a short stay from England. The heat went off and we huddled under blankets and drank champagne, one New Years Eve!

"While I was President of the National Council of the Alumni Association of the Conservatory across Canada, we held our annual meeting here. We had a delightful luncheon at which Spencer Clark spoke and told the guests much of The Guild's history.

"I usually only had to ring the day before to engage my favourite room, # 328 in the old wing, for the week-end. Now at least two weeks is needed.

"It is wonderful to be living and working still with music here at Corycliff. A number of my students come from out-of-town and stay at The Guild, after a two-hour evening lesson, instead of driving back that night. One of them says he likes to jog around before breakfast.

"I always feel Rosa Clark is especially sympathetic to the musical activities. She studied and sang under the tutelage of Arthur Blight who was greatly in demand at the Toronto Conservatory of Music as it was first called. I am thrilled to see the fine sculpture in The Guild grounds, now with the bas-relief portraits of Sir Ernest MacMillan and Dr. Healey Willan. Both of them encouraged me in my early student days."

Other Crafts

The Guild Inn's Craft Shop
From the Breithaupt Hewetson Clark Collection
University of Waterloo

Tooled Leather

Leather crafts were produced at the Guild of All Arts and often sold in their shop. Crafts people, such as Walter Goforth, used various methods to create leather products.

The grain of leather runs along the backbone of the skin. Long strips were cut to make belts. Other belts were made by cut sections pieced together. Patterns on leather products could be traced using a pencil point, leather tool with a tapered point or any pointed instrument. Cutting leather is easier when it's damp.

Carving sloping edges compresses the leather and darkens the colour. The burning in of a pattern is accomplished by using a wood burning tool, which is best done on dry leather. Gouging out a design cuts and removes portions of the leather. To create an engraved relief design, it can be pressed down into the leather from the front or from the reverse side, pushed up. A metal stamp is used to impress a design into the leather for repeated shapes and the pattern is imbedded by hitting the stamp with a wooden mallet.

An embossed leather design needs something to fill the hollows to prevent the pattern's collapse. The design is created on the back then filled with a special filler. Metal mold plates with an engraved design are heated. The leather is placed between two plates and the design embedded by the heat.

Leather can be dyed but sometimes the colour fades. For an even appearance, use cheesecloth, or a sheepswool puff. A circular motion gives the dye an even look on leather, and for a woodgrain effect, use long strokes along the grain.

The Guild produced leather items such as book marks, bracelets, belts and small purses. Two women, Muriel Burnaby, and Martha McCully, are listed as leather tool workers.

Walter Goforth at work tooling leather
From the Breithaupt Hewetson Clark Collection
University of Waterloo

Walter Goforth—Leather Tooling 1911–1998

During the 1930s Walter Goforth was employed at the Guild of All Arts for $3.00 per week. He worked in leather tooling producing such things as bookmarks, belts, small purses and bracelets. In January 1934, an article in the Weekly Sun by Mrs. Smith of Englehart, mentions an item of leather. "Among the leather goods...a pair of baby shoes made of pink leather with gold lacings...not only beautiful workmanship but cozy comfort too."

Walter had other artistic talents. In the 1930s there was a shed behind a farmhouse on Kingston Road and Scarborough Golf Club Road. In an article by the Reverend Glenn Tenpenny "From the Vestry" at Washington United Church, he states, "...He (Walter) had heard that the shed...had been the previous church building on the site. In 1885, when the new church had been built, the farmer had volunteered to remove the old frame building and reconstruct it...as a shed on his farm." Walter sketched the building, and later did a painting of how the church would have looked in the 1840s. This painting hangs in the narthex of the current Washington United Church.

Walter spent his childhood on a farm on Markham Rd.. This property was later sold and became Cedarbrae Golf Course. He had a good sense of humour, was an inventor, a storyteller, and a church choir member. As well he had a wonderful imagination and was always creating new games and ways to have fun.

Hallmark Cards employed him in their creative department where he worked for many years. He continued spending time at the Guild Inn. He was known as a man who disliked throwing anything away. One time he went to an auction and bought a "bunch of sticks." This was a dismantled weaving loom which he reassembled. A friend, Jane Coulter, set up the weaving using binder twine and the neighbourhood children made placemats.

Walter spent his remaining years in Norwood, Ontario, where he was a choir member of Norwood Church. He died on November 4, 1998. His three paintings of Washington Church still hang in the building as a memory to this creative man and his many talents.

Silver Smithing

In the past centuries silver products were made by hammering shapes on tree trunks, cut short, so the craftsman could sit on a stool. Rich patrons and the church received these silver products designed especially for them, sometimes with their initials or family crest. At that time a silversmith apprenticed for seven years. London, England set the fashion mode for silver work designs.

Silver's most desirable quality is its malleability. It is a soft metal, pliable for shaping, stretching and yielding easily to various shapes. In later years rolled silver sheets were available, the pattern cut then soldered to produce cups, bowls, teapots, etc.

Hollow vessels can be produced from discs then shaped by spinning them on a lathe. Silversmiths used this lathe in which a piece of metal is held between shaped tools and spun. Thicker metal requires less speed in turning and the craftsman works to produce the desired shape while the lathe is turning. To lessen the friction on silver while turning, oil covers the disc.

To add decorative touches, handles, spouts etc., silver pieces are soldered on after the initial shape is created. Lids were attached, for example to a teakettle, using a small hinge. Feet were added to support the kettle that brewed water.

Today the art of silver smithing has almost disappeared due to the high cost of labour, modern materials and modern manufacturing processes.

Silver teapot made by Arthur Neville Kirk
while at the Guild Inn
From the collection of The Guild

Silver dish made by Arthur Neville Kirk
while at the Guild Inn
From the collection of The Guild

Silver cross made by Arthur Neville Kirk
From the collection of The Guild

Silver Smith Arthur Neville Kirk
From the collection of The Guild

Arthur Neville Kirk—Silver Smith

In 1935 the Guild of All Arts announced an exhibition of silver work by an internationally famous silver smith, Arthur Neville Kirk. During that summer at the Guild he conducted a school in the art of designing with silver, gold and enamel.

Arthur had been commissioned to create items in silver for European cathedrals and for the Royal family. He had been an instructor at the Artisan Guild in Michigan, U.S.A., and in London, England at the Cranbrook Academy of Arts and the Central School of Arts and Crafts.

While in Toronto for the exhibition of his work, he stayed at the Guild Inn. Several items produced by him, while there, were a silver candy dish, a tea pot and a silver cross.

Wrought Iron and Metal Shop
From the Breithaupt Hewetson Clark Collection
University of Waterloo

Wrought Iron

For weapons, primitive man wanted a harder substance than wood or stone. Experiments were conducted on melting ores and over thousands of years an important craft was created. In the middle ages craftsmen fashioned armour, grilles, implements and utensils in beautiful designs. In the era of the Guild of All Arts, wrought iron was used for home decoration in English, Spanish and modern styles. Wrought iron is a useful and almost permanent feature.

The definition for wrought iron comes from to “wreak”, to bend or twist. Pure iron is only moderately hard and can be shaped when it is red hot. Cast iron liquid, produced by extreme heat, is brittle and can’t be bent or shaped when it solidifies because of the carbon content. Hammering when it is hot will break the cast iron. Iron rusts easily.

At 700 degrees Celsius the iron is red hot forming a pliable substance called a “bloom”. The smithy can hammer on this and shape it to the desired design. In Sweden archaeological evidence of cast iron was found from the middle ages for the period 1150 to 1350. Cast iron was produced with a method using a water-wheel and large bellows in a smelter furnace. One product that was made then were cannon balls. Later cast iron cannons were made to fire the cannon balls.

In the wrought iron shop the Freeman family, the father John and his two sons, crafted items for sale and for use in the inn. This family created interior railings costing from $3.85 a foot up to $6.50 a foot. Exterior railings of cast iron with handrails, ranged from $30.00 a pair up to $38.00 a pair. With bronze handrails the cost was $52.00 to $58.00 a pair.

Fireplaces could be enhanced with intricately designed utensils. Fire dogs were designed to hold a grate for the wood, ranging in height from 18 1/2” up to 24”. These were finished with polished brass or a black finish and priced from $33.00 to $47.00 a pair. The burning fire eventually caused the fire dogs to crumble as the fireplaces were usually in constant use. Wrought iron screens were also finished with polished brass which could be decorated with a family crest. Fireplace tools, a poker, shovel, wood holder and a container for ashes were available from $1.75 to $15.00.

Ornamental items included lamps, lanterns, electrical fixtures and candle sticks. A delicate arch lamp was a fanciful design of curves and swirls priced from $50.00 to $300.00. Wall brackets for electric lights were designed in the style of ancient lanterns. Ceiling fixtures were a plain design or reminiscent of church fixtures.

The workshop was in a separate building on the south-west side of the Studio building. This building had been converted from a three car garage.

Today the work of wrought iron for railings and decorative items continues as a commercial and artistic venture. The gates at the entrance to Guildwood Village and in the Guild Inn Park are samples of wrought iron work done by craftsmen, an ancient art that survives with constant attention to prevent them rusting away.

Eric Aldwinckle—Printing
1909–1980

In 1951 "Graphik", a German periodical review, stated, "It is not without charm to become acquainted with typically Canadian creative advertising through the medium of a personality like Aldwinckle." However, Eric Aldwinckle was born in Oxford, England and came to Canada at age 15 when he stayed with relatives. He was influenced by the painting style of the Group of Seven artists. Although listed as a printer at the Guild Inn, Eric was also an artist.

As a book illustrator he used pure egg tempera which is a dry paint pigment mixed with egg yolk. He was skilled at calligraphy and did posters, medallions and painted portraits. After teaching at the Ontario College of Arts until 1942, he joined the Royal Canadian Air Force in eastern Ontario. His unique skills led to camouflage painting on military equipment. From there he became an official war artist. In this capacity he completed 126 war paintings. At the end of the war, Eric returned to the profession of an artist.

Pearl McCarthy of the Globe and Mail acknowledged his work on August 2, 1952. She stated, "Aldwinckle's life and his art are unified...designs a letterhead, there is a suggestion of contemplative thought...plus a quiet dignity...He designed the medal awarded by the Massey Foundation for architecture...murals for the veterans hospital, Sunnybrook Park...was Graphic Art Director for the Stratford Festival (1955-59)...designed the great seal of Canada..."

In 1980, at age 71, Eric Aldwinckle died in Toronto.

Raffia

Definition: Fiber used especially for making baskets and hats that is obtained from the stalks of the leaves of a Madagascar palm tree.

The Guild of All Arts worked with raffia to produce coffee bottles. The raffia was wound tightly around the neck of the bottle, attached to the cork. These bottles were made in various sizes from 16 cups to a half cup.

There were many other uses from woven raffia fabric. Things such as a woman's bag, tea cozies, slippers, table runner, cushions and dinner place mats, could be made from raffia. Another suggested use was a raffia egg stand that could hold five eggs. A pattern sheet mentioned using raffia to form a pattern on Hessian fabric or coloured canvas, to make shopping bags or a writing case.

Corycliff

Corycliff Lodge
From the collection of The Guild

Cory on the Cliff (Corycliff) 1912–1997

Corycliff had a remarkable history and unfortunately, a dismal ending when it deteriorated beyond repair. It was built in 1912 as a summer residence on the top of Scarborough Bluffs for a family named Burton. However, they did not give the building its well-known name.

The next owners, Mr. & Mrs. A. Roy Courtice and Mr. & Mrs. Colin Campbell, named their new summer dwelling. Ada Courtice, mother of the owner, called the building "Cory on the Cliff" after her father Reverend Cory, a famous Methodist minister. Roy Courtice's wife Rody, knew the Group of Seven painters and sometimes painted with them. Colin Campbell was married to the sister of Roy Courtice, and was a superintendent of insurance for the Ontario Government. In 1934 Rosa and Spencer Clark purchased Corycliff.

The structure was originally a two storey frame house with wooden shingles on the exterior walls. A screened-in veranda, on the south side, overlooked Lake Ontario. Fieldstone pillars supported the verandah that was several feet above the ground. These stones also formed the foundations of the building. The open space under the verandah was for storage. To keep animals out, this space was enclosed with wire. On the south east side, wooden steps led onto the verandah to the main entrance on the south side. The roof, on the east and west sides, extended over the exterior walls. There was a field stone chimney. Below the cliff was a beach area which in 1979 had almost disappeared.

The second floor had four rooms. In later years, it became a guest lodge with a bathroom for each room. When Rosa and Spencer purchased Corycliff they did minor alterations by adding a bathroom and replacing the rough boulders on the fireplace with natural split stone.

More changes occurred in 1947 both to the exterior and interior. Wire mesh was laid over the walls on the exterior then stuccoed in white. An enclosed sunroom replaced the verandah and its roof became a balcony with iron railings. A two car garage was added on the north side of the building. The double hung sash windows were replaced with picture windows, with side openings.

One day during the renovations while Spencer was ill, he noticed that the original wooden steps needed replacing. He designed a stone terrace and new steps.

During WWII Corycliff was taken over by the Ontario Government and in 1942 became known as "H.M.C.S. Bytown II". Rosa, Spencer and the four children, were forced to move into the city of Toronto until 1947. Fifty WRENS were trained here as radio operators. The grounds later became known as Scarborough Hall, a specialized military hospital.

When the Clarks returned to the Guild Inn, more renovations were done to Corycliff to change it from a home into a guest lodge. One of the renovations was to add a wall covering. The handwoven material, made on the Guildcrest looms, was woven of jute binder twine in a check pattern. This was the same material that had been applied to the walls of the Oak and Coral dining rooms. This material, and the wall, were destroyed in 1985 when Corycliffe was renovated as a conference centre.

In 1956 a new kitchen was added at the north side of the building and second story extended over this new room.

In 1967 Corycliff became a school for crafts. The arts group offered weaving and spinning courses, rug hooking, ceramics, copper enameling, decorative folk art and painting instruction. After two years the Guildcrest School of All Arts and Crafts needed more space and moved to larger quarters. Eventually this group moved to the Fraser Mansion now know as Cedar Ridge Studio.

Corycliff then became a staff cottage and studios. At one time three piano teachers resided there, one was Virginia Knott.

The end of Corycliff occurred in September 1997 when bulldozers moved in and demolished the building. Only photos and memories remain of the 85 year old building that was once alive with visitors, various students and the Clark family.

Guildwoods Hall and Guildwoods School

Guildwoods Hall
From the collection of The Guild

Guildwoods Hall (1920s to 1964) and Guildwoods School (1935)

On October 1st, 1934 Rosa M. Hewetson Clark purchased a large house near the Guild Inn from Highland Creek Ltd., in trust for Guildwoods School. She had two mortgages on the property as this property was priced higher than other surrounding properties. Previous owners appear to have been Thomas J. Ford and Jessie May Washington. Lakeshore Land Co. and the president, Cecil White, also appear to be involved with this property.

The large building, a suitable size for a school, may have been a summer lodge. In 1935 Guildwoods School was opened for residential and day students. The school "...is set in wide places, far from feverish marts." The building was heated by an oil burner with a modern air-conditioning plant.

A brochure gave details of the school itself, the area and the close proximity to the Guild House. There was also mention of the children's playhouse, the log cabin and the Great Elm tree. Children would be led into self-knowledge, self-control and self reverence for a full life. "...By means of creative work and play, the development of thought and skill, by means of self-government and social co-operation, each individual develops that sound integrity and sense of values which lets him or her to live usefully and abundantly under whatever social and economic conditions confront him."

Health was stressed with unlimited fresh air and sunshine, exercise, outdoor projects, wholesome food and adequate rest. Parents were asked to keep their children away from "minor public epidemics" and children showing signs of a cold or other disorder, would be isolated.

Year I was a nursery programme including Eurythmics and a tea party. There were prayers, Bible study, work and play projects with outdoor activities.

For students in the Upper School, as well as regular courses for Junior and Senior matriculation, there were other required courses. They had classes in English, Bible studies, household science for girls, shop for the boys, science, music, Eurythmics, arts and crafts. The lower school was taught reading visually, phonetically and by the

Winnekta method. Games and projects taught numbers and there was daily French conversation. A daily Bible story was sometimes acted out by the students.

Younger children were also accommodated at Guildwoods School. They learned modeling, art, drama, stories and conversational French. "...the five year old child is further initiated into the joy of living and his individual aptitudes and intents developed."

Outdoor activities occurred in fields and woodlands surrounding the school. A student could play tennis and basketball. In the winter students enjoyed ice skating, tobogganing, skiing and snowshoeing. Other cultural activities were available in nearby Toronto where students would be exposed to museums, art galleries, music and drama.

The school year opened on September 18, until December 19, 1935, when it was closed for Christmas recess. School re-opened January 6, 1936 until Easter recess March 21. The third term opened April 7, 1936 and closed on June 12.

School fees were broken into three categories and the student was registered for the full year. Day school was $225.00 for the year including a $15.00 registration fee. Full residence was $600.00 plus registration of $75.00. Five day residence was $475.00 for the year including registration of $55.00. Outstanding fees for the first term, apparently for four students, totalled $140.45. For the second term for six students, and payment from H.S. Clark (Spencer) of $280.00, the total was $708.34. However, it appears one student requested a refund of $140.00 and H.S. Clark had overpaid. The parent of one student was credited with the school fee of $140.00 for doing accounting.

The staff consisted of four full-time teachers and six part-time for cultural studies. Boris Berlin, a well-known musician, gave piano lessons. Rosa and Spencer were members of the Board of Advisors.

Crestwood Motor Service supplied a taxi service to drive students to and from the school. In February 1936 charges for this service ranged from 25¢ per ride up to 85¢. From the school to Highland Creek, to take the Misses Ogdens home, the charge was 60¢. For the month of February the total charge was $13.40.

Peerless Laundry received cheques to pay for their services. A cleaner named Schwartz received a cheque for 88¢ to clean the school. A note on the back of the chit indicates that payment should have been $1.00. Crestwood farm supplied the school with poultry. Highland Dairy received payment probably for milk and other dairy products. School supplies were purchased from the T. Eaton Co. and the Robert Simpson Co.

The school director, and also a teacher, was Isobel Brown Thomas. Cheques issued to her from September to December 1935 amounted to $340.00. Beverley Richardson received four cheques totalling $60.00. She may have been a teacher and possibly the sister of Blanche Richardson. Blanche was paid more than Beverley at a total of $85.00 for the two terms from September to March. She also is not listed as a teacher.

Boris Berlin taught music and for this was paid a total of $154.62. It appears that he was at the school from September to December 1935.

An advertisement was placed in the Toronto Star in June 24, 1936. A one-time ad of twenty-six words cost $1.30. However, the school only lasted for one year, from September 1935 until approximately March 1936. In the Guild files there is no record of cheques beyond this date.

An account from the Guild Inn for school charges was from January 6 to 12, 1936. Room and board for Miss Johnson and Miss Campbell cost $12.65. Children's meals at 25¢ each totalled $20.50. There was an unspecified charge of $1.45 to Mrs. Thomas.

In 1936 The Canadian Bank of Commerce, which was the bank for Guildwood's School, the deposit slip had information not included in today's slips. As well as bill denominations from $1.00 to $100.00, there was a listing for: gold; silver; coppers; and cheques. Cheques that were cashed at this bank often had a stamp on the back cut with a picture of their tall building, with the date on which it was cashed. On the front of each cheque is a 3¢ postage stamp. This stamp was purchased to raise funds for the war effort.

After WWII members of the Canadian Armed Services found refuge at Guildwoods Hall. It accommodated 30 patients suffering from nerves shattered by their war experiences.

During the 1950s Guildwoods Hall was renovated. Then in 1964 the building was demolished for the Sir Wilfred Laurier high school.

Osterhout Log Cabin

The Osterhout Log Cabin
From the collection of The Guild

The Osterhout Log Cabin

Mystery and myth surround the building known as the Osterhout Log Cabin. It was built sometime in the late 1700s or mid 1800s by an unknown person.

The first myth is that the builder was a surveyor named Augustus Jones who built it for his survey crew. The story is that the crew travelled by water from York (Toronto) and lived there during the week, then travelled by water back to York on the weekends. However, the crew would have had a difficult climb up the 122 metre high (400') clay cliffs.

Military personnel were often assigned duties of surveying and road construction. They built log structures quickly using squared logs with dovetail joints for stability. This cabin is not built that way.

Round logs were used to build the cabin with square-notched corners. This method suggests that it was built by a homesteader as a temporary residence until he could afford to build a better home for his family.

Squared logs fit tighter and require less chinking (filling gaps). If an immediate shelter was required, round log structures were erected and the gaps filled with wood slabs or stones packed with oakum (loosely twisted hemp or jute soaked with tar), moss, clay or animal dung. A final coating of clay and lime was wet-trowelled to the gaps. This cabin was chinked with wooden slats and covered with mortar.

A final note on this myth regards the crew. Augustus Jones' crew of eight men worked 79 days without a break surveying townships on the north side of Lake Ontario from River Trent (Bay of Quinte) to York. In his notes, Augustus mentioned that his crew lived in tents.

The next suggested builder is William Osterhout, a farmer settled in Scarborough. As a member of Butler's Rangers from the Niagara District, he petitioned John Graves Simcoe, the Governor, for a land grant and received Lot 14, concession C in Scarborough. Unfortunately, petitioners for land could not choose the area they wanted.

Six years later, in 1805, apparently without living on the land, William Osterhout sold the property. It was purchased by Alexander McDonell of York and there is no record of a building on the property. However, land transfer documents only gave information about the land whether there was a building on it or not.

Alexander McDonell was also one of Butler's Rangers, a lieutenant who moved to York in 1797. In 1811 he was summoned to England by the Earl of Selkirk and returned the following year, 1812, as a Colonel. In 1818 he built a distinguished residence in York at Adelaide and John Streets. This suggests that he would never have built a small one-room cabin for his family.

The cabin property was only a small part of Alexander McDonell's land holdings. He owned over four thousand hectares of prime land in Ontario. In 1834 the cabin property was sold to Duncan Cameron.

Duncan Cameron owned the property for less than a month. He paid £100 (one hundred pounds) in October 1834 and in November sold this property for the same price to John Ewart of Toronto.

John Ewart was an architectural designer and designed many of the buildings in York. However, a man of his wealth would not have lived in a one room cabin in Scarborough nor designed such a structure. There is no record of his residence in Scarborough although he owned this property until 1845.

The next owners were homesteaders who might have built this style of cabin. James Humphreys, an Irish immigrant, brought his family to Canada in 1824 and lived with his wife's family, the Richardsons, in a log cabin. The Humphreys family later moved to Lot 8, Concession I where they opened a tavern. They purchased the cabin property from John Ewart in 1845 and in 1858, James sold the property to his son William. In 1861 the cabin is first recorded on the census report. William Humphreys, his family and three other people are listed as residing in the cabin. In 1909 the property was sold to Graham Chambers.

During the early 1900s, ownership of the land is recorded as changing several times. The cabin is mentioned in a land transfer in June 1912. The land was sold by Edward Duncan to Allison Burton of Toronto but he retained a right-of-way and the land containing the log cabin.

In 1934 new owners, Rosa and Spencer Clark, bought the property and incorporated it into the Guild of All Arts.

The cabin is 6.5 metres long (21') by 4.8 metres wide (15.75') and began as one room with a loft. The round logs were square notched at the corners with a tie log in the centre to prevent the log ends from sliding apart. These tie logs were also floor joists (small beams to support a floor). Little technical skill is required to build this type of structure.

Inside the cabin is a fireplace with the chimney inside the walls. Built of bricks and mortar the chimney extends through the loft then out through the roof. It is 1.56 metres wide (5') inside the cabin, and 1.26 metres (4') high and was a source of heating as well as for cooking.

In the 1920s an additional section was added to the cabin, on the west side for modern sanitation facilities and water. A concrete walkway on the north side of the cabin, covered by an extension of the roof, led to the annex. Then in 1965 a new log wall was built to enclose the north porch creating a hallway to the annex.

In 1965 the chimney was blocked up and the fireplace became unusable. The loft was insulated and electric baseboard heaters along with modern fluorescent lights were installed.

In 1984 repairs were again necessary as the cabin required new chinking, a new shingle roof and replacement of the second log on the east side. In 1986 the cabin was restored to its original form and the annex and north porch removed and the water disconnected.

On July 23, 1942 there was an advertisement for rental of the log cabin during the summer months. Mentioned was the large fireplace, running water, a bathroom and a kitchen. Rent was $2.75 per day, $16.50 per week and $60.00 per month. In 1943 a retired prospector, Joe Mason, lived in the unheated log cabin. He was a poet who wrote about Canada's far north and enjoyed taking snow baths as recorded in an article on March 22, 1943 in the Telegram newspaper.

From early 1950 to late 60s, a resident of the cabin was Lucy Doyle. After she left, the cabin was used for a brief period of time by the Guildcrest Studio of Arts, then was occupied by sculptor John Byers. Elizabeth Fraser Williamson was the last sculptor to use the cabin.

In an article by Lucy Doyle she mentioned that Mrs. Humphreys had planted lilac bushes that were, at the time she lived there, tree high. Black cherry trees and an apple orchard was also nearby.

The television series, "The Whiteoaks of Jalna", was filmed at the cabin. It also appeared in the movie, "It Seemed Like A Good Idea at the Time". Today the cabin sometimes is still used for television productions. In 1978 the cabin was sold to new owners.

The Metropolitan Toronto and Region Conservation Authority, with financial support from the Province of Ontario, purchased the cabin from Spencer Clark. In 1980 Scarborough designated the cabin as the Osterhout Cabin, a historical building. In 1994 an investigation was conducted by digging a test pit for historical artifacts that would define the age of the cabin. In 1996 a report on the findings associated with the cabin became available from Metropolitan Toronto Parks and Culture Department.

Although the truth about the cabin's builder is unknown, it stands as a reminder of Scarborough's history for future generations to experience how early settlers and those who came after them once lived. Preserved on the grounds of the Guild Inn, the Osterhout cabin is an integral part of one of Toronto's historic parks where visitors can wander freely and relive the past.

Lucy Swanton Doyle
1880–1971

For eighteen years Lucy Doyle lived in the log cabin at the Guild Inn. As a messenger and later a reporter for prominent city newspaper, the Toronto Telegram from 1896 until 1930, she was considered the best woman journalist of her day. However, in later years while living at the Guild, she produced very few articles and became an eccentric annoyance.

Lucy Doyle was born in 1880 in Des Moines, Iowa, United States and in 1902 both of her parents, Charles and Lillian, were killed in an automobile accident. She was the third child of four. Two older brothers were Howard Cameron and Charles Homer and her younger sister, Leila Gertrude, who died in 1940.

When she was 14 years old Lucy made a request of an aunt who lived in Weston, Ontario to give her brother Homer, her sister Lelia and herself, a home. She promised to find a job to support them. At age 16 she became a messenger girl for the Toronto Telegram and went on to become a well-known writer. She began as a proofreader, and later worked at general reporting, then became a drama critic and editor of the Women's Page. Under the pseudonym of Cornelia, she wrote about Toronto's social news.

Canadian history and society were some of her passionate interests. She wrote about them as well as about her travels, her exploits and about the little-known facts of history.

With a memory that could recall an abundance of facts, she was a fascinating storyteller on historical, political or social events. One evening she visited the wealthy Mrs. Ambrose Small, wife of the owner of a famous downtown theatre. The following day Ambrose Small disappeared. To this day his body has never been located and the mystery remains unsolved.

When covering a society wedding on Long Island, New York, an event which was barred to the press, Lucy discovered a unique way to get the facts. The ceremony took place on the banks of a river. She hired a boat where she and a photographer hid in the shrubs while the guests gathered. When the ceremony began she ordered the photographer to stand waist-deep in the water to take pictures. With the boat in full view of the wedding party and guests, she made notes

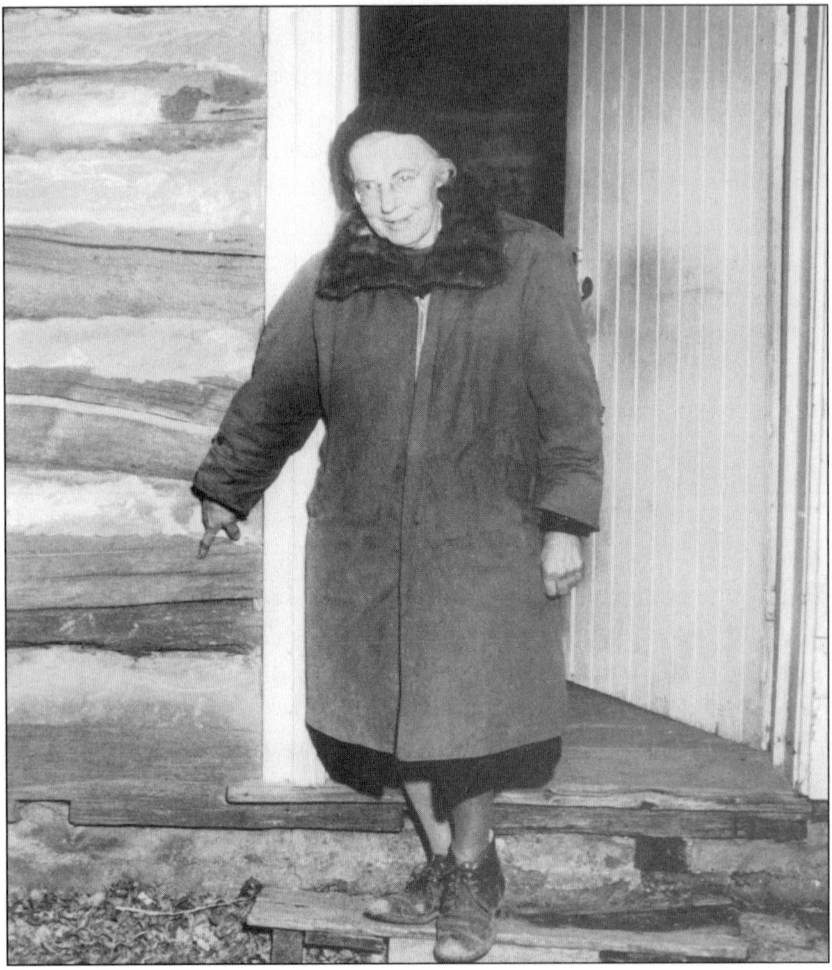

Lucy Doyle
From the Breithaupt Hewetson Clark Collection
University of Waterloo

about the event, including discriptions of the guests' fashions. Her determination and tenacity rewarded her with an article for the newspaper.

She covered all the tours of the Prince of Wales. One time when leaving his ship, he asked, "Where's Lucy?" She once climbed aboard his ship from a tender to be the first one to get an interview. At the Prince's newly acquired ranch in Alberta, Lucy hung over the fence to attract his attention and obtain an interview.

Her story wirtten during World War I about an incompetent munitions maker, forced the government to change the process for accepting contracts.

In 1930 Lucy left the staff of the Evening telegram and as a member of the International Daughters of the Empire, (I.O.D.E.) attended a conference in London, England as a Canadian representative. Three of the delegates were presented with medals by King George V. Lucy was one of them.

In Scarborough, Lucy Doyle lived in a school house in a valley which she and her brother purchased in 1933, which is now part of the University of Toronto Scarborough Campus. The building had been known as SS No. 7, the West Hill/Highland Creek School. It had been built in 1870 on what was a picturesque country road that later became Old Kingston Rd. A large frame building, it had tall, church-like windows, a gallery and a belfry. The land cost the School Trustees $100.00 and $1300.00 to erect the schoolhouse. A backhouse (outdoor toilet) cost $20.00 to build. In 1923 the building was sold and became a dance hall. Later it was used to repair motorcycles then became a private dwelling.

In April 1951 Lucy burned the spring grass around her home. A neighbour, Mr. F. Harbutt saw smoke coming from her property and ran to give assistance. He found her slumped over her typewriter, carried her out thus saving her life. The fire rapidly spread and before the arrival of the fire department, burned down her home and everything she owned including all the notes she had kept for a book on the Duke of Wales. The only things remaining on the property was an outside toilet and a telephone pole. Her brother's old car was jacked up on blocks. Friends were glad to have the eccentric woman live with them until they tired of her independent habits and she wore out her welcome. Often she returned to her property to sort out her papers which had been saved from the fire, stored in her brother's car.

She missed talking by telephone with her friends and applied for the installation of a phone in the car. The Bell Telephone Company refused to install a phone. Undaunted, she researched the telephone company's franchise agreement and discovered that they were required to install a phone in a dwelling if the occupant could pay. An election act defined a dwelling as a place where the owner ate and slept. So she moved into the car where she slept sitting upright, picnicking during the day.

With legal papers in hand, Lucy visited the telephone company office. She besieged the president with her demands for a telephone. After firmly refusing, he finally relented and a telephone was installed in the car. In a sense, she was the first person to have a car phone.

At 71 years old, Lucy's income was the basic Old Age Pension. When the Toronto Women's Press Club gave her a cash gift, she used it to attend a historical convention in the United States. When she returned she stayed with friends then made a visit to the Guild Inn. Rosa Clark invited her to stay at the Guild Inn for several months. It was a visit that lasted eighteen years.

Lucy's stay at the Guild Inn was intended for the purpose of writing a history of the property. However, the only things she wrote was an article on the great elm tree and a short history of the log cabin. She did contribute articles to the Scarborough News and later, when Guildwood Village was established, wrote a column of Guildwood News. However, she did not contribute to the expenses of the cabin.

Her expenses for rent, taxes, heat, hydro, telephone and food, were paid by the Guild Inn. Other companies where Lucy had purchased products, contacted the Inn for payment. This added to their financial problems of paying their own bills.

Rosa and Spencer often invited Lucy to the dine at the Inn and sometimes the staff took meals to her. Other times she cashed cheques at the front office, or the craft shop, without money to cover them. Spencer personally paid her telephone bills which often included long distance calls.

At times Lucy sat in the lobby of the Inn asking guests to give her a ride. Many complaints were lodged by the guests who did not appreciate these requests, and it had a bad effect on business. Other times she took copies of the newspapers without paying. The Inn also absorbed expenses for her personal entertaining. For a short period of time, Lucy lived in the kitchen-sitting room at Corycliff but she preferred the log cabin. This caused more expense.

To make her more comfortable the log cabin had to be renovated. It cost $4,000.00 to insulate the ceiling and bathroom, build a log wall to enclose the north section of the open porch, and install a heavy-duty electrical system for the electric heating. Two small fires in the cabin necessitated the need for electric heating.

Scarborough Council often held meetings at the Guild Inn. Lucy considered herself still part of the press corps although she was no longer an accredited member. She attended these meetings and annoyed elected members. When she could not be restrained from attending these meetings, the council held their meeting elsewhere which meant a loss of revenue for the Guild Inn.

Rosa Clark often took her to auction sales and allowed her to purchase books. Of course it was Rosa who paid for these purchases. Lucy also borrowed books from her friends which were returned only after her death. Mrs. Mavor Moore, wife of the famed theatrical personality, loaned her some furniture, which was never used, and remained stored in the Annex of the cabin.

One of Lucy's habits was to sit up late at night making notes from the books she was reading. Some of these notes were illegible and these were stored in the basement of Corycliff. These slips of paper became badly mildewed and could not be saved. There was talk of all the manuscripts she was working on but writing was never completed on paper, only in her head.

In her last years she could be very affectionate one moment, then suddenly became antagonistic. She had been moved to the Guildwood Villa Nursing Home where her outbursts of temper and noisy tantrums required her to be transferred to a mental institution in Whitby, Ontario. While residing in Guildwood Villa, she threw a cup of tea at a nurse who had walked into her room at the wrong moment. She was recovering from pneumonia in the Villa because there were no rooms available in the hospital, and had been ringing for the nurse as her roommate had fallen out of bed. For this, a doctor

Memorial Cairn to Lucy Doyle
On the property of University of Toronto, Scarborough Campus
From the author's collection

said she was demented and sent her to Whitby. Without funds to pay for residence in the Villa, the Guildwood Village Association contributed $100.00. From the Villa she was moved to a Bobcaygeon nursing home where she died on March 18, 1971.

Although Lucy Doyle never produced sufficient quantities of work for the Guild, Rosa and Spencer Clark allowed her to stay for eighteen years. They knew she had no where else to go and could not, in good conscience, force her out. This was part of their dedication to the betterment of living conditions for others, although costly to themselves. The Scarborough Campus offered to buy the two acres of property where the schoolhouse had been, but Lucy preferred to leave it to them in her will.

A stone cairn and plaque was constructed on the property she once owned by Mr. F. Harbutt, the neighbour who had saved her life. The cairn was dedicated on October 10, 1973 in memory of Lucy Swanton Doyle, indomitable reporter and journalist who was once the best in her field. It stands there today, close to Old Kingston Road, set back against the trees.

The Cottages

Top cottage	*Originally the baker's cottage* *Used by Elizabeth Fraser Williamson*
Bottom cottage	*Originally the Gray's cottage* *Used by Michael Clay* *From the collection of The Guild*

The Cottages

At one time there were four cottages on the Guild Inn property, which had been located on other sites and moved in the late 1950s. In 1955 three cottages were moved from the area known as Livingston Park. They were designated on a site plan as the Foote cottage, the Gray cottage and the Dick cottage where they stood on the south west side of Corycliff Road in the Duncan block. A fourth cottage designated as the Arnold cottage was moved from the edge of the cliffs to the area where the first three cottages had been. The fourth cottage, known as the Ward cottage, had been located there prior to 1954. Several other cottages including the English and Munro cottages, were to be renovated at their current location. None of these cottages remain there today.[1]

The cottages were occupied by Guild Inn staff and their families. It was not until the 1970s that they were occupied by resident artists. In the 1980s in two of the unoccupied cottages vandals broke in and started fires.

Two cottages were occupied by sculptors, Elizabeth Fraser Williamson and the other Michael Clay. In 1968 the cottage later occupied by Elizabeth was known as the baker's cottage. It was 723 sq. feet with a closed-in front porch and contained three bedrooms, a kitchen, bathroom, and a living room. Her cottage was used as a showroom for her work and living quarters. She also sculpted in the Osterhout log cabin and gave lessons there.

The cottage occupied by Michael Clay was much larger. It was 1098 sq. feet with a sunporch, it had seven bedrooms, a bed-sitting room and a bathroom. Previously the cottage had been used by staff waiters.

In 1992 the cottage near Corycliff was near total collapse. The roof had fallen in. In 1993 a report done for a meeting of the Management Committee considered they were not an historically important part of the history of the Guild as they had been moved in during the 1950s. They were not part of Metro's subsidized housing

---

1 *The name designations on these cottages are estimations and may not be accurate as the photographs were not labelled.*

Top cottage — *Ward's cottage, was at the front of the Inn*

Bottom cottage — *English's cottage*
From the collection of The Guild

policy yet Metropolitan Toronto continued to pay the costs for two occupants, a maintenance of approximately $13,000.00 a year.

As well, the cottages were below building code regulations. It would cost approximately $50,000.00 for each cottage to be repaired plus yearly expenses for maintenance. The report states that the previous owners, Rosa and Spencer "*...had a right to invite resident artists and to support them financially. Now taxpayers money is being spent to support two individuals whose presence on-site has never been approved by the present owner of the property.*"

In December 1975 the two vandalized cottages were demolished, and six months later the last two cottages suffered the same fate. Elizabeth Williamson had moved to Livingston Lodge. Michael Clay had moved out long before the decision and the cottage had been occupied by a non-artisan resident.

Arnold's Cottage
From the collection of The Guild

Top cottage *McNeill's cottage*
Bottom cottage *Munro's cottage*

From the collection of The Guild

Reprint from Guildwood News—November 7, 1963

"Queen's University has no more precious corner than the "Edith and Lorne Pierce" Room. It is the home of their rare collection over the years of Canada's most priceless records of people who have tried to put her into words.

About forty years ago Canada's beloved historian lived in the summer cottage at The Guild Inn next to the Log Cabin. It was here Dr. Pierce began his editing of the Ryerson Press series on the Makers of Canadian Literature. So intrigued was he with Judge Riddell's story of "William Kirby", he resolved to do one himself. He wrote it in the Cabin and declared it was his best work. When Thomas Bowie's statue of St. Francis was erected on the Guild Inn lawn, Dr. Pierce made one of his most masterful speeches at the unveiling.

To link Lorne Pierce's happy days at Guildwood, a precious corner of the Guild's library has just been set aside. In it are a blue and gold "Makers" series, a copy of Pierce's "William Kirby" and three copies of the latter's "Golden Dog." There is the latter's 1877 edition published without permission by a New York pirate. Side by side with it is the 1897 edition with a Kirby preface."

The Studio

The Studio
From the author's collection

The Studio Building

On the property purchased by Rosa Hewetson in 1932, a stable once held polo ponies of the original owner, Colonel Harold Bickford. The stable contained box stalls for the ponies with a second level above for a hayloft. A second building was a two car garage with a chauffeur's apartment above. These two buildings were joined together to form the first section of the Studio.

The stable was called the south wing and became the workshop for pewter and copper. The garage, designated as the west wing, became a woodworking shop.

An addition was constructed to the east side of the building for the craft shop of exhibits and items for sale. A corner chimney was built in the east wing and connected to the pewter shop.

In the south wing, above the pewter shop, the weaving studio wove material, some of which decorated the walls of the dining rooms. On the second floor of the east wing was the batik studio. Crafts people working with tooled leather, block printing and ceramics were also located here.

In 1957 another addition was added to the Studio, the north wing which became the woodworking studio. Then in 1960 the Studio was renovated as a meeting room for conferences, wedding receptions and other similar functions. A floor plan of the second floor of the east wing shows a batik studio and in the south wing and a weaving studio. Part of the second floor, in the north wing, is an apartment for an employee. In the other sections a room is for brides and a smaller room for grooms. A serving kitchen was added to the west side of the Studio in 1963.

Today, the studio accommodates various meetings and the apartment on the second floor is still used by a former employee.

Wishing Well—erected in 1935
Restored in 1994
From the author's collection

The Pottery Kiln

The pottery kiln was built on the grounds of the Guild Inn by Mr. Eardley in 1937. He was from a well-known English ceramic family in Staffordshire. Most of the Guild's original pottery pieces were fired in this kiln.

The pottery kiln
From the collection of The Guild

The Control Station

Originally this station stood on an island near the front entrance of the Guild Inn. A uniformed staff member inhabited the station and regulated the flow of traffic, as well as accepting money when a fee was charged to get into the Guild Inn grounds. It was moved nearer to the gates but was removed due to difficulty for cars to enter or leave, and was no longer staffed. The station was not preserved and eventually rotted away and demolished from lack of use.

From the author's collection

The Gazebo

The gazebo once stood in the south-east garden. It was a mail-order do-it-yourself kit which was first installed on the Clark's property in Huntsville, Ontario and later moved to the Guild Inn. Vandals destroyed the fragile structure of the gazebo and it could not be rebuilt In 1987.

From the collection of The Guild

The Maze

In 1705 a cedar maze was planted at Hampton Court in England, for Queen Anne. This maze was replicated at the Guild of All Arts in 1948 in the garden overlooking Lake Ontario. It lasted until 1981 when it was removed and replanted, to allow space to build the Greek Theatre.

In a map showing the placement of the seating for the Greek Theatre, the maze is estimated to have been 150' wide at the front. On each side the estimated size was approximately 75' long and across the back 55' wide.

From the collection of The Guild

Children's Playhouse

This was situated on the south-west side of the Guild Inn. It was designed as a miniature French Canadian chalet with a winding staircase. Outside, children enjoyed a playground of a jungle gym, teeter-totters and slides.

The playhouse was moved by the youngest daughter of Paul Breithaupt, Rosa's brother, to her property, possibly in Guelph, where her husband was teaching.

From the Breithaupt Hewetson Clark Collection
University of Waterloo

The Duncan Barn
From the collection of The Guild

The Duncan Barn

As with the log cabin, there are no documents about the date the Duncan barn was built. A 1942 site plan records the existence of the barn. It is assumed the barn was located on property owned by Edward Duncan which stood on the north-west side of the log cabin.

The barn was probably used as a horse stable and possibly for carriages. A grain chute opened on one side and stables were in the rear.

In 1996 an inspection of the barn showed that the main floor was divided into three rooms with what appeared to be a pantry at the rear. A ladder led into the loft above. From the building detail, inside walls were finished, electric outlets available, so the barn could have been used as a craft studio rather than a stable.

Further investigation revealed that the barn could have been approximately 60 years old. At the front of the building other foundation stones suggested a previous building at this site.

The barn because of its dilapidated state, with the rear of the building collapsing, and holes in the roof where racoons had made a home in the loft, was demolished in March 1996.

From the collection of The Guild

Back to the Inn

Aerial view of the Guild Inn
From the Breithaupt Hewetson Clark Collection
University of Waterloo

Back to the Inn

After World War II the Guild Inn could no longer afford to subsidize their craftsmen. Some returned to the Inn but others had relocated their studios but continued to send their work for sale in the craft shop. The Inn became a place for visitors and non-resident craftsman to stay, primarily during the summer months. Renovations were made and more accommodations added. In the early 1950s a Metropolitan Regional government decreased thirteen municipalities to six and took over administration of the areas around Toronto to harmonize services. Taxes on the 500 acre property increased dramatically. In a period of seven years they increased from $3,000.00 per year to $70,000.00. Rosa and Spencer Clark could not afford this increase and were forced to sell the majority of their property. Rather than just sell to land developers as with many Scarborough properties, Rosa and Spencer planned a unique community called Guildwood Village, around the Inn. This ensured that their dream continued.

Visitors from all social levels visited the Guild Inn. Movie makers also used the property for location shots, especially the Osterhout log cabin. Prime ministers visited the inn, as did provincial premiers and foreign ambassadors. Movie stars, musicians, all found the Inn to be a unique place to see while in Toronto. Royal visitors included Queen Juliana of the Netherlands and Grand Duchess Olga, sister of the last Tzar of Russia. A film made in 1980 on the history of the Inn was narrated by Lorraine Thomson for CBC television. It was requested by the Ontario government to help publicize the Inn and was shown on TVO as well as other stations. Lorraine Thomson interviewed A.J. Casson and Sorel Etrog.

Rosa and Spencer were also involved in other areas of the arts, outside of the Guild Inn. He was involved in preserving Toronto's heritage buildings and was part of a group of citizens who were instrumental in saving Old City Hall from demolition. Other buildings which he could not save, are preserved in the architectural pieces erected in the garden of the Guild Inn.

Spencer was the president for the Memorial Fund of Albert M. Campbell, a former mayor of Scarborough. He initiated a project to erect a sculpture, a bronze entitled the "Hand of God" located in the garden on the south side of Borough Drive near Scarborough Civic Centre.

To commemorate 100 years of engineering at the University of Toronto, Spencer chaired the committee. A contemporary sculpture "Beccas H" by Robert Murray, was erected in front of the Galbraith Building on the University of Toronto property. Although he received credit for these projects, Rosa often helped with her knowledge and love of art. In 1978 both received the Scarborough Award of Merit for their many years of contributions to the public in the area of the Arts.

With the Canadian Tourist Association of Canada, as Chairman of the Historical and Cultural Committee, Spencer helped preserve other historical artifacts in Canada. In Sibbald Park on Lake Simcoe, the property which contained several buildings, Eildon Hall and St. George's church was put up for sale. The stained glass altar windows in the church were made by the daughters of John Graves Simcoe, a former Lieutenant Governor. This area is now known as Sibblad Point Provincial Park.

Working with the historical committee, he was able to help preserve the longest covered bridge in the world located in Hartland, New Brunswick. Instead of being demolished to create space for a highway, the bridge was moved to a new location.

Artists, musicians, sculptors and other crafts people continued to work and visit at the Guild Inn. A cabinet maker, Herman Riedl, was part of the Guild Inn for 32 years. Sculptors lived in two of the cabins, taught in the log cabin, or worked in the sculpture cabin.

In 1962 an art fair was held at the Guild Inn by the Women's Auxiliary of Scarborough General Hospital. Entrace fee cost 50¢ to get in which included a cup of tea and a draw ticket on an Eskimo carving or a handcrafted tray. This fair had been held elsewhere in previous years and grown so much that the Auxiliary needed a more spacious location. Painters, sculptors such as E. B. Cox, potters, metal art workers, leathercraft artisans, weavers, spinners and a textile printer, displayed and demonstrated their skills and work.

Alan Bowie, son of sculptor Thomas Bowie, worked at the Guild Inn for three years, first as a dishwasher and then a busboy. He remembers when meals were delivered to the Studio from the man kitchen by Volkswagen vans. He'd hide in the bushes and help himself to the delicious honey buns. One of his jobs keeping logs burning in the fireplace in the main dining room.

When Margaret (Bowie) Beckman worked in the kitchen she remembers a staff member making a huge mistake. The meals were cooked in the main kitchen, transported to the Studio in the vans and placed on steam tables. Everything was always in the same place. This staff member decided it would be better to switch things around a bit. Where the gravy usually sat, he put the butterscotch sauce, and the gravy where the sauce usually was. Other staff, unaware of this change, served as usual. Diners got butterscotch sauce on their potatoes and gravy on their icecream. That staff member was severely reprimanded and for future meals, serving dishes were put in their usual places.

Many staff members were brought from Europe, their passage paid by the Guild Inn. Most did not speak English very well and stayed only for a year. During the time that Tom and Betty Bowie lived on Woodvale Avenue, Betty gave informal English lessons in her home. One way the staff learned English was to read comic books.

The staff was like a large family and the young people often had many impromptu parties. A Christmas party was held and later a New Year's Eve party, with rent paid to the Inn for use of Guildwood Hall and the Studio.

In 1981 Alan and Margaret held a surprise party for the 50th wedding anniversary of their parents. They booked a dinning room and were surprised at their reception. The staff were surly and there was only one small bar. Then Spencer dropped in to let them know he would be down later to join in the celebration. Instantly the attitude of the staff changed and another bar was added. He appreciated and remembered with kindness those who worked for him and were part of the Inn's history.

In 1982 the Guild Inn celebrated its 50th anniversary. Sorel Etrog organized a "Contemporary" outdoor sculpture exhibit from August 3rd to October 14th. Thirty-five artists created art work especially for this show. A medallion commemorating this anniversary was designed and a few of these still exist as a valued memento of a historic achievement in the arts.

Rosa Melvina Breithaupt Hewetson Clark
From the collection of The Guild

During the summer months, onsite sculptors invited visitors to view their work. Elizabeth Fraser Williamson opened her cabin to visitors where they could watch her at work and view her finished collection. Sculptors like Dorsey James, Tom Feenstra and Gerd Untermann, who at various times worked in the sculpture cabin, invited weekend visitors to view their work. The craftshop which for 30 years was under the capable hands of Miss Blanche Kenny, gave visitors an opportunity to support the Inn and its crafts people by purchasing their work. The shop was later managed by Margaret Sideway.

It was less expensive to stay in the older section of the Inn. In the mid 1970s it cost $70.00 per night. However, the windows were not screened and surprises occurred. Nancy MacDonald, former housekeeper for 18 years, remembers hearing a staff member scream. One of the cleaning staff had entered a room and encountered an unpaid guest. A large racoon had climbed in through the open window and made himself at home in a chair. Unwanted, he promptly exited through the same window.

One couple loved the old wing of the Inn. They always requested the same room, Number 327, because as artists they could stow their equipment in an alcove under the roof.

Operating the Inn was still a financial struggle. Visitors didn't help when they stole the towels bearing the Guild Inn logo. The passing years brought health problems to both Rosa and Spencer.

In 1975 at the age of 87, Rosa had a stroke. She was confined to a wheelchair after the stroke and unable to participate as fully in the activities of the Guild Inn as she had always done. Paralyzed on her left side she was unable to use that hand. Fortunately her speech was not affected and her mind functioned well, but she tired easily.

Spencer suffered from crippling arthritis. However, the pain was alleviated by regular visits to spas at Abara, near Venice, Italy. Swimming 20 lengths in his pool before breakfast also helped. But both he and Rosa knew that their years of owning and managing the inn were coming to an end.

For ten years he had tried to convince the government of Ontario and Metropolitan Toronto to buy the property. In a statement to the press he said, "Before I die I want to make sure this place is going to continue. It's my life's work. Every bit of it has been a labour of love." (Sunday Star, September 28, 1980). Finally, in May 1978 Metropolitan Toronto council voted to purchase the property.

Not everyone on council voted to acquire the Guild Inn. Three councillors voted against the purchase. Mel Lastman, Irv Chapley and Alan Redway, who did not represent Scarborough, were against the deal. Twenty-five other councillors agreed and Metro and the Province of Ontario bought the Guild Inn property for $8 million. The final agreement was reached in 1979 with Spencer remaining to manage the property, without payment for his services, for five years. Two years later, in 1981 at the age of 93, Rosa Breithaupt Hewetson Clark died.

Guildwood Village

Gates of Guildwood

These gates were forged in England in 1839 for Toronto's Stanley Barracks. The barracks were demolished in 1953 and the gates rebuilt on their present site, at the top of Guildwood Parkway, in 1957 as a grand entrance to Guildwood Village.

Guildwood Village

Guildwood Village is a planned community built around the existing, major trees rather than destroy them. Aerial photographs were taken during the winter to show the location of the trees. Some were moved for the construction of water mains and pipes, while others were tunnelled under. Wiring was placed underground instead of being suspended from lighting and telephone poles which would spoil the look of the community. Streets were designed to slow the speed of traffic. Also included in the plan were three miles of park walkways. A unique concept, Guildwood Village was "...a whole community being built by public spirited citizens, for something more than the usual business and profit purposes."[1]

As an engineer, Spencer Clark had a vision and practical outlook of what Guildwood Village should be. The entrance was to be more than just another road into a subdivision. He wanted to create the atmosphere of entering into a superior residential area rather than just moving from one subdivision to another. His study of the garden villages in England, Bournville, Port Sunlight, Hampstead Garden, and the United States, Chatham Village, and Shaker Heights proved to be very beneficial. The heart of the village should be a "village green". The garden cities had a central area apartments, a high school, and a shopping centre which were surrounded by homes in various styles. Other uses would be special schools for nursery children and a health centre. At one time two automobile service stations were located in Guildwood Village on Guildwood Parkway. One of these sites is now a small park and the other slated for construction of townhouses.

Plans proposed two churches, a community meeting and recreation centre, a library and professional building. Pedestrians were encouraged to walk around their neighbourhoods, the walkways had a pleasant appeal with shorter routes between other streets. Included in the design were play areas for the children with access to the schools from the streets, along attractive footpaths.

---

1 *Scarborough Enterprise Novemeber 22, 1956.*

Many things were to be avoided in planning this community. No homes should have the front and back property on a main road. Easy access sould allow for the maintenance of city-owned property without undue inconvenience to the community for things such as weed and bush control, and garbage collection. Ample lighting must be installed to reduce the loitering of undesirable persons, to promote the feeling of security at night. In May 1955 a draft plan of the subdivision was sent by the Planning Consultant Company to the Ontario Community Planning Branch of Ontario.

Seven building companies were employed by Guildwood Developments Ltd., a company Spencer Clark was instrumental in originating, to create a variety of house styles. Rosa's son Russell Hewetson was one of the directors of the development company and also vice-president and general manager of a local construction company, Crescent Construction. House frontages would range from 60' to 100' wide. Prices were from $22,000.00 up to $100,000.00 and the entire village developed over a five year period. The area for development was approximately 400 acres equal to the size of the towns of Mimico and New Toronto (now part of the city of Toronto).

Guildwood Parkway, which was once Eglinton Avenue East, was to be a wider street than required. Similar thoroughfares were usually 60' wide but this road would be 96' wide so a grass median could be installed. As this road descends sharply down the hill from Kingston Road, it was necessary to turn its direction and lengthen it to make the grade easier from the highway to the lower level.

In 1957 model were homes constructed on Toynbee Trail and contestants of the Miss Canada Pageant were taken on a tour. These became part of the first 344 homes priced at $23,000.00 each.

Transportation to this community was a major factor and well served by various methods including the TTC (Toronto Transit Commission) and Gray Coach buses. Commuter trains (which later became GO (Government Ontario trains) stopped at the Guildwood station and the (now defunct) Gardiner Expressway interchanges were planned too. Spencer's wish for a grand entrance at the top of Guildwood Parkway was also achieved.

In 1957 gates from a demolished military barracks were re-built at the entrance. They had been forged in England in 1839 and

Russell Hewetson—son of Rosa Hewetson Clark
From the collection of The Guild

shipped to Canada in 1841. The gates were installed in the City of Toronto at the main military facility of New Fort, later called Fort Toronto. This was later named the Stanley Barracks which was demolished in 1953.

Street names related to history, the arts and family connections of Rosa and Spencer Clark. One street was named after a longtime member of the Toronto Rotary Club who had owned property in this location.

Robert Watson McClain dressed himself in silk hat, tails and formal dress and took a white horse to the Royal York Hotel. It was his 90th birthday and he rode his horse into a freight elevator up to the main ballroom. His picture astride his horse appeared in the Globe and Mail. To commemorate his ownership of land within the village, he was asked to suggest a name for the street. McClain Avenue might become confused with McLean Avenue in the Beaches so that name could not be used. His suggestion to call the street "Uncle Wat Boulevard" was abbreviated to become Rowatson Road.

On Livingston Road a skating rink was once used by the staff from the Inn. This space is now occupied by the St. Ursula Catholic School. This area from Toynbee Trail to Guildwood Parkway was once a large apple orchard. Before Guildwood Village, the houses in the area had no steps at the front door, which was often high above the ground. Entry was through the back garden because adding a front step and entrance would double the owner's taxes. Until then, the houses were not considered to be fully built.

Several designs were suggested for the Guildwood Village's crest. One showed a seagull over ripples below the sunshine, and standing on top of this was a squirrel and a pine tree. Another design was a graphic-style seagull in a shield with various things on top. A third was of a seagull over the lake with trees on the shore. The design chosen became the seagull over the lake, squirrel and pine tree.

At the official opening ceremony of Guildwood Village, Bob Hope, the well-known comedian, cut the ribbon. Several people who bought homes in the Village themselves became well-known personalities. Pierre Berton and Charles Templeton owned homes here, in a street off Toynbee Trail.

A small house on Toynbee Trail was once owned by Margaret (Neilson) Usher. It was a very narrow lot and existed until the 1990s. Russell Hewetson stopped developers from demolishing it until Margaret was ready to move. A modern house sits on the narrow site today.

"Let us mingle the Beautiful with the Useful."

After the Clarks

Rosa and Spencer Clark
receive the Scarborough Civic Award of Merit
May 14, 1979
From the collection of The Guild

After the Clarks

Rosa Clark died on Tuesday, July 7, 1981 at Scarborough Centenary Hospital, at the age of 93. The funeral service was held on July 13, 1981 at Yorkminster Park Baptist Church, conducted by Dr. John N. Gladstone. In his reflections on her life, Dr. Gladstone said, "She was devoted to her husband, children and later, to her grandchildren and great-grand-children...She pursued beauty and strove for excellence...Neither Rosa nor Spencer ever surrendered their visions. They never let their idealism be swept away by a tide of cynicism...I think of Rosa's infectious sense of fun. This was the other side of her...How she could laugh at life's absurdities." Rosa is buried in Mount Pleasant Cemetery.

Although Spencer Clark retained management of the Guild Inn through his company Ravenna Guild Inn Ltd., he and the new owners did not have similar plans. Two years after the Province of Ontario and Metropolitan Toronto bought the Inn, they announced they wanted to turn it into a public park. There would be a wine garden/food pavilion and possibly a MacDonald's restaurant. Other plans included eliminating the path from the Inn to the top of the bluffs. Spencer and local residents were outraged at this disregard for the Inn's history and arts centre. The new owners had set up a task force with plans for the Inn without any input from Rosa and Spencer.

In 1983 the Guild's Board of Management issued their own plans. They would create a luxury hotel, at the cost of $17.5 million, including a wharf and picnic area at lakeside. Inside a fitness centre would be an indoor pool and sauna. There were also plans for theatre and concerts at the Greek Theatre. Metropolitan Toronto approved the plan and began a search for public money.

After Ravenna Guild Inn Ltd. company ended its management of the Inn, June 1983, a Board of Management took control. Their tenure ended in January 1985, when Delta Hotels took over the management of the Inn. At the beginning of Delta Hotel's second year, February 1986, Spencer Clark died of a heart attack.

Feeling quite well, his last excursion was to go out to dinner, but as he walked along, collapsed on the sidewalk. He was rushed to Toronto General Hospital but died before he arrived. He was 82 years old and died on February 11, 1986. The funeral service was held at

Herbert Spencer Clark
Photo by Karsh
From the collection of The Guild

Yorkminster Park Baptist Church, and he was buried in Mount Pleasant Cemetery.

In a tribute by Sorel Etrog, "For a short while Spencer's dream came true. The task is left now for us to make his dream a reality."

Dr. Gladstone also reflected on Spencer's life. "Spencer Clark was a communicator of joy. The irresistible exuberance of his personality, the passion for beauty in nature, in art in all its expressions, and in people all lifted us from the drab, flat plains of life, to the very heights at times of ecstasy. He enjoyed life, and he was good to be with. It will be a sadder place without him...What is said of Christopher Wren...could very well be said of Spencer Clark: "If you seek his monument, look around you, and you will find signs of it"...I think first of Spencer's vitality. How alive he was...He had many more ideas—some of them farfetched...but he had more ideas jostling in his mind in five minutes than many people have in a lifetime...I think next of Spencer's curiosity. He maintained to the very end of his life a child-like sense of wonder...There was no need for Spencer to buy the book, *Who's Who in Canada*. He could have written it...He had an extra-ordinary encyclopedic knowledge of people—because he loved people...Spencer was no back-seat personality. He loved publicity, he loved leadership, he rejoiced in the honours that were given to him."

Delta Hotels managed the Inn for two years followed by C N Hotels Inc. C N Hotels were to develop the Inn in accordance with plans from Metro. In 1988 the C N Hotels were sold and their lease was not renewed. In September 1988 Giant Step Realty Corporation was leased the Inn for a period of 99 years. However, Giant Step only lasted until 1993 because their vision for the Inn created a disastrous impact for the community.

The proposal by Giant Step would change the Inn from 96 rooms into a massive hotel with 437 rooms. To do this sculptures and architectural remnants would have to be relocated, including the Sculptor's Cabin. In their place would be parking. To make room, mature trees would also have to be removed. On the roof of the parking garage, two stories high with 344 spaces, there would be three tennis courts. The west parking structure would have 395 spaces. On the lake side of the Inn there would be two new wings, once again requiring removal of sculptures and architectural structures.

The new west wing would be ten stories high with 204 suites, a cultural centre and a conference centre. The existing seven floor wing would have an eighth floor added. The new east wing would be eight floors high with 124 suites and a single storey recreation facility. Between the main Guild Inn building and the proposed west wing, would be an enclosed walkway.

The Guildwood Village Community Association were given a copy of this plan. A special committee was formed to reply to the proposed plan. During 1990 the special committee analyzed the developer's report and prepared their answer. On February 21, 1991, the committee made a resolution that the plan "not" be accepted by Metropolitan Toronto.

Reasons against the proposal included traffic problems. Scarborough Transportation and Planning did a traffic study on the number of vehicles using Guildwood Parkway and Galloway Road, feeder roads from Kingston Road. During peak periods, 8:00–9:00 a.m. and 5:00–6:00 p.m. on a week day, traffic flow was approximately 800 vehicles and roads easily accommodated them. In between these times there was a low volume of traffic. The proposed development would dramatically increase traffic at all times of the day. It would necessitate the widening of Guildwood Parkway from two lanes to four which would destroy the quiet quality of life for residents and imperil the lives of students crossing to schools.

Another concern was continued public access to Guild Inn grounds. There was unrestricted access at any time and Giant Step would be given the authority to set "reasonable rules and regulations" for public access for security reasons. Then there was the destruction of trees in the Carolinian forest.

The removal of approximately 450 mature trees was necessary for construction of the additions. There was a proposal to shore up some trees close to the foundations which could damage their roots. For each tree removed two new ones would be planted. However, it would take many years to replace the beauty that was lost.

Waterfront was also a major concern. There were fears that a marina would be built. While not mentioned in the proposed plan it was an interest to generate more tourists to the hotel and might be considered later by Giant Step.

No time limit was placed on the construction of this proposal.

Would Giant Step stay until the completion of the additions? Financing of this proposal could be easy to obtain on the existing buildings. There seemed to be no regulations to stop the developer from selling the lease without the consent of the owners or abandoning the Inn leaving the government with the mortgages to pay. Metro and Scarborough would not amend the zoning bylaw which allowed for this massive project. The bylaw was finally amended in 1993 to allow only an open space for a park and minimal expansion of the Inn.

Would this massive hotel, in an isolated area from entertainment, be a success? No record existed of any similar project by Giant Step that had been successful. In a list of Metro hotels, the Guild Inn was rated sixty-seventh. The proposal would relocated the rating of the Inn into seventh place, larger in banquet space and rooms than either the Prince Hotel and Sheraton Parkway East. Both these hotels are situated on major roads. This large hotel complex in a residential area is unprecedented. An economic downturn cancelled the proposal and Giant Step walked away from the lease leaving unpaid rent and taxes.

In 1993 Giant Step closed the Guild Inn. The gardens had been neglected and the Inn was in desperate need of a caring touch. Metropolitan Toronto Parks took over and the gardens were restored and once again received excellent care. In July 1993 a new management company, Ifield Hotel Association received a lease to operate the Inn, which they still manage today. The Guild Inn serves delicious meals, but unfortunately the patrons are not able to see the cultural influence as the artists and sculptors are gone. The dream of Rosa and Spencer Clark has died but the watchdogs, Guildwood Village Community Association and the Guild Renaissance Group hope to change that.

An opinion article in the Scarborough Mirror, June 2, 1993 says it all. "The Guild Inn needs the kind of suitor that is in short supply these days: someone of means who cares more for preserving something unique than for increasing the bottom line."

The Sunday Star, September 28, 1980, is worth mentioning again, where Spencer Clark was quoted as saying, "People make things so complicated...There's a simple answer for all this. Just keep it going."

The Guild Inn Today—2000

The craftsmen, artists and sculptors are gone but the beauty of the Guild Inn remains. Visitors still enjoy a delicious meal in the dining room, or in the warm months, under the canopy on the patio. Architectural structures still stand in the well-kept gardens high above Lake Ontario. It's a popular location for conferences and weddings, with receptions in the Studio or in the main building. Rooms are still occupied by visitors who enjoy its unique setting and quietness.

For three months during a low-activity time for guests, January to March, the Inn closes for repairs and renovations. On an August weekend the Scarborough Arts Council holds its "Arts Naturally" exhibition and sale. In the summer of 1999, theatre groups performed plays at the Greek Theatre. In December there is a Christmas Carol evening and lights are arrayed on the trees in the north garden.

What is the future for the Guild Inn? Visitors and residents would like to see the return of crafts people and sculptors working on the grounds and in the sculpture cabin. Many studies have been done on how to make the Inn a "paying venture." Plans for the Inn have been included in Toronto's waterfront project that spreads over 25 miles of lakefront. The Guild Inn is proposed to be converted into a community arts centre with an outdoor theatre. On the waterfront, a bicycle trail at the base of the bluffs would extend from Etobicoke to Rouge Beach, and there would also be a port for a ferry or water taxi.

Whatever the future holds the Guild Inn's watchdogs, the Guildwood Community Association and the Guild Renaissance Group, will ensure that nothing is destroyed in the process. The main building has been designated as "historical" as well as the log cabin. The dream continues to be a contribution to the arts, and a memory to be preserved that will last as long as the building and sculpture gardens remain.

Sculpture Garden

Sketches by: **Hugh Walker**

From his book: *The Spencer Clark Collection of Historic Architecture*

Sketches used with the permission of Hugh Walker

Stonemason Arthur Hibberd
From the collection of The Guild

The Sculpture Garden

The city of Toronto was tearing down its history and the memories of its buildings would have been lost except for the intervention of two visionaries, Rosa and Spencer Clark, both members of the Ontario Historical Society, who wanted to preserve the history. Unable to save entire buildings, they erected fragments in their garden at the Guild Inn. They enlisted the help of various engineers, architects and a stonemason, Arthur Hibberd, one of the last stonemasons capable of this enormous task.

Spencer was often at the demolition site of these historic buildings. He had remnants carted away and over the years erected them in the gardens. It was a slow job to ensure that these structures would last for a very long time. The foundations were large with the joints mortored, sometimes pinned and copper flashing was added where needed. These structures are estimated to endure for thousands of years, but a few have needed repairs. Over 60 of Toronto's historic buildings, and some from other areas of Ontario, are remembered through these structures. The buildings are gone but memory of them has not perished with their destruction.

Entrance gates to the main grounds of the Guild Inn. The ironwork is from Gibson House, 5 Dale Avenue, Rosedale and the lights from Sunnyside Boardwalk, Toronto.

The Greek Theatre
From a postcard

The Greek Theatre

An eight columned marble structure was erected with parts from the Bank of Toronto to commemorate the 50th anniversary of the Guild Inn. This was called the Greek Theatre and in 1981 was the only one of its kind in Canada. The eight columns and corinthian capitals, arches joining the columns, were saved in 1966 from the demolition of the Toronto Dominion Bank which stood at the corner of Bay Street and King Street. The bank had been built in 1912.

Future plans for the Greek Theatre included tiered seating for an amphitheatre. This necessitated removal of the cedar maze which would be replanted around the theatre. There was to be eight tiers of seats in front of the theatre with steps up each side and at the back. Behind the theatre would be change rooms with two public washrooms. A grassed slope filled in the back of the change rooms. The steps and stage area were built from poured concrete and not relocated from a demolished building.

The Greek Theatre was erected by stonemason Arthur Hibberd but the amphitheatre was never built. Today an open area remains behind the theatre bordered by cedar trees, where performers gather before their shows. The audience brings their own chairs or sit on the grass. The plans are still available for the amphitheatre and perhaps someday may be used to build the seating, yet the view across the grass frontage of the theatre adds to visitors' enjoyment as they stroll down the main path to the top of the bluffs.

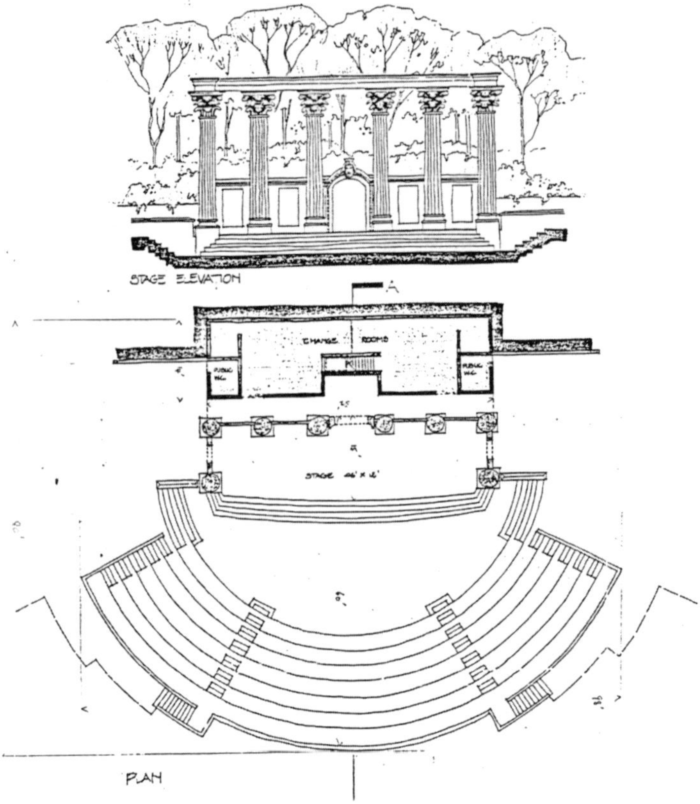

Proposed Amphitheatre

North Garden

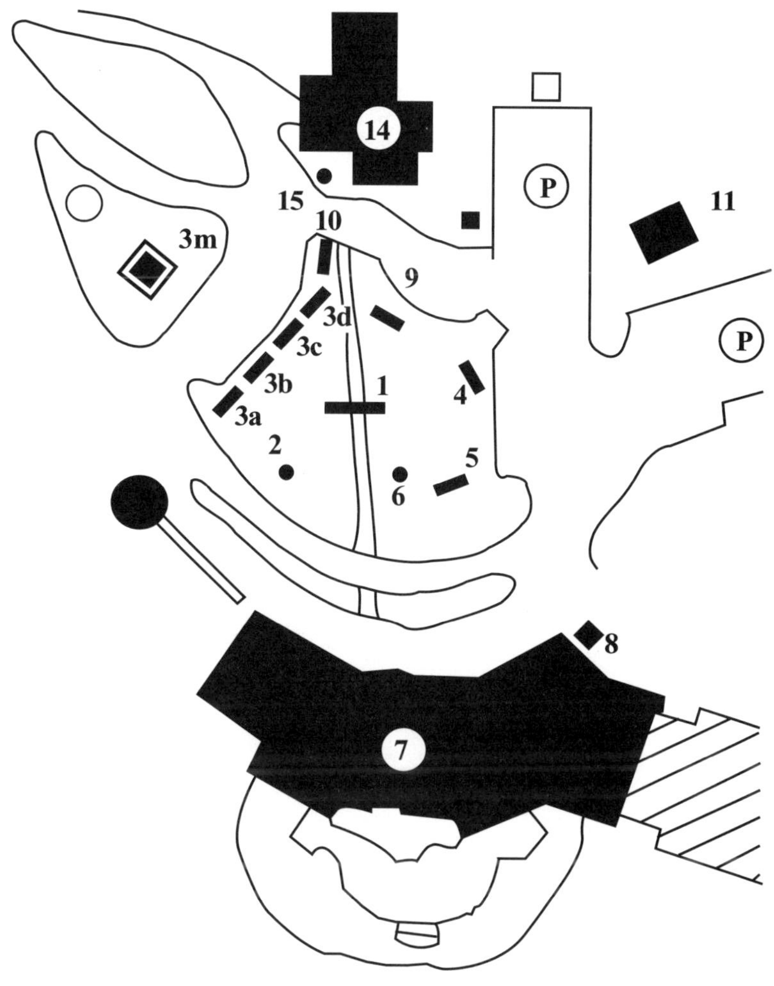

North Garden

1. **Bankers Bond Building -four Ionic Capitals and columns**

This building, built in 1920, stood at 60 King Street West. It was occupied by the Bankers Bond Company Limited until 1941. In 1936, until 1948, Barclays Bank occupied a portion of the building. In 1958 it became known as the Canadian Building, occupied by an insurance company. The National Bank of Canada also occupied space. The Bank of Montreal owned this building until it was demolished in 1973.

Ionic Columns – Indiana Limestone

2. **Ravenna—Sorel Etrog**

Ravenna, 1965-66 60" high

3. **Bank of Montreal panels**

Animal Bas-Relief Panels
3a Buffalo
3b Walrus
3c Beaver
3d Polar Bear

The six limestone animal panels were designed by Jacobine Jones[1]. The walrus, bear and buffalo and were above the King Street entrances. The other three panels (see # 9 and 10) of the skunk, wolves and beaver, were above the Bay Street entrances.

Beaver

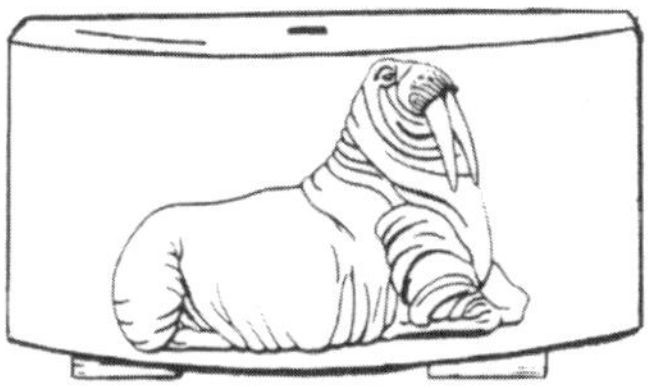

Walrus

Polar Bear

1 *Put on Her Mettle* The Life and Art of Jacobine Jones by Natalie Luckyj, Penumbra Press 1999.

3m Panels of the provinces

Ontario	-	designed by Frances Loring
Quebec	-	designed by Frances Loring
British Columbia	-	designed by Jacobine Jones
Nova Scotia	-	designed by Donald Stewart

The finial on top of these provincial panels is from the entrance gate to Victoria Park, Niagara Falls, Ontario.

Construction on the Bank of Montreal building began in 1937 but stopped in 1939 because of World War II. The building was not completed until 1948. Six sculptors were commissoned to create the panels. Ten panels are in the north garden, four in the south west garden and four in the sout east garden. The twelve provincial panels were on the walls of the recessed entrances. The bank of Montreal building was demolished in 1972. It is now the site of the First Canadian Place.

4. Temple Building—entrance and panels

Red Sandstone from Sackville, N.B.

The first highrise building in Toronto was built in 1895. The Temple Building was ten stories tall and in 1901 an elevator was installed. A full-blooded Canadian Indian of the Mohawk tribe, Chief Oronhyatekha, was known as the "Builder" of the Independant Order of Foresters, a group that occupied this building. The moosehead is a symbol of this order, although the spread of carved antlers was not preserved. The carvings were created using red sandstone from Sackville, New Brunswick. In 1970 the building was demolished, replaced by a 32 storey office building.

5. **Two angel panels**
North American Life Insurance Building

The building was erected in 1932 at 112 King Street West. The angel panels were located near the top of the building, the exact design reversed for the second one. However, in reversing the design, the sculptor reversed the map of North America. Florida is shown in the west and Alaska in the east. The building was demolished in 1976, and the site is now part of First Canadian Place.

6. **Space plough—Sorel Etrog**
acquired in 1981 (see section on Sculptors on Sorel Etrog)

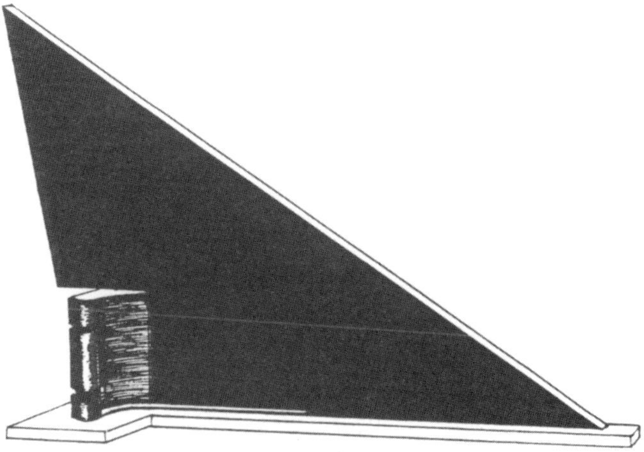

Space Plough, 1981 139" high

7. **The Guild Inn**

8. **Planter—1 Hayter St.**

9. **Bank of Montreal—Bas-Relief Panel**
Skunk

10. **Bank of Montreal—Bas Relief Panel**
Wolves

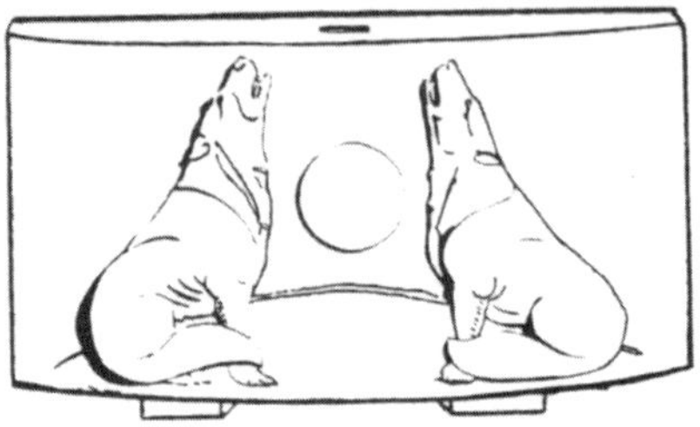

11. **Sculpture Studio**
(See section on Sculpture Studio page 91)

12. **Pottery Kiln**

13. **Wishing Well**
    erected in 1935—restored in 1994

14. **Studio**
    (See section on Studio page 223)

15. **Mobius Curve—Michael Clay**

This sculpture stood upright on end while it was being carved but the artist's concept was for it to be on its side. The Mobius Curve is based on a piece of paper forming a single twist, defined by German mathematician August Mobius. Spencer Clark commissoned this sculpture in 1982. The sculpture was carved from a 15 ton block of Indiana limestone.

The round inground garden was a window trim from the University College. There is another one on the west side of the Inn. These were obtained when the college was renovated in 1973.

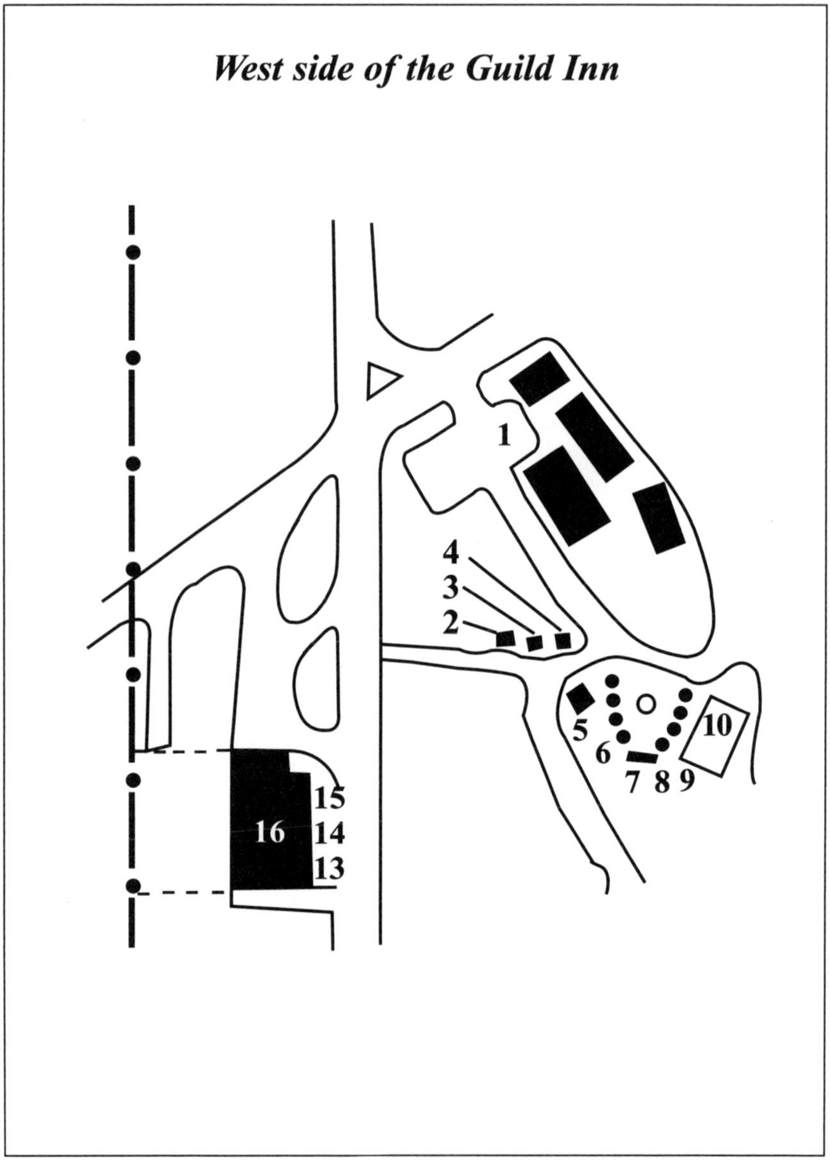
West side of the Guild Inn
1
4
3
2
5
6
7 8 9
10
15
16
14
13

West side of the Guild Inn

1. **Guild Inn Service Court**

2. **Engine House No. 2**

The 18' long sign was cut from 10" thick stone, from Toronto's second firehall. The building was built in 1871, with an addition in 1904. It was demolished in 1968.

3. **Stone cutting machine**
fly wheel and drive mechanism

Stone mason, Arthur Hibberd, donated this machine to the Guild Inn in 1976 when he closed his business. This machine was used to cut up large blocks of stone up to 20 tons in weight, using steel shot and water, then diamond-studded teeth were used.

4. **Belfry and bell**

The school, Section No. 23, originally known as O'Sullivan's Corner School, was built in 1873. Later the school was named Victoria Park School and was located where the 401 is. A former premier of Ontario, George S. Henry, attended the school. The building was used as a school until 1946, then demolished in 1964.

5. **Smoke house**

The smoke house was built for the exclusive use of the Inn's chef to smoke their meat and fish. It burned down in 1989 and was rebuilt.

6. **O'Keefe Brewery Keystone**

The corner of Victoria and Gould Streets once had a brewery building which was built in 1840. In 1862 Eugene O'Keefe purchased the brewery from Hannah and Hart brewers. This site is now part of Ryerson Polytechnical Institute, as the original building was demolished in 1976.

7. **Banting House mantlepiece**

Sir Frederick Banting, co-founder of insulin, built his home in 1928 at 46 Bedford Road. He lived there until 1933, and the building was demolished in 1966. Frederick Banting was a close friend of Spencer Clark.

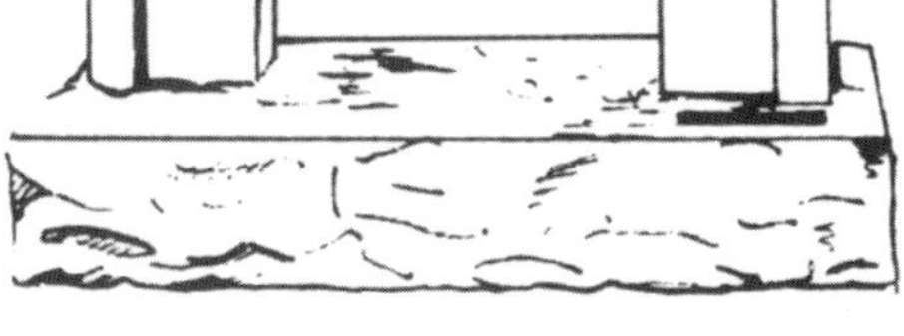

8. **Pineapple Finial**

This piece is from the Provincial Paper Limited building at 388 University Avenue, and built in 1930. It was demolished in 1968 and the site is now occupied by a building known as 400 University Avenue.

9. **Medical Building—University of Toronto**

two ionic capital columns—white terra-cotta

In this medical building, built in 1904, Dr. Frederick Banting did his research on insulin. Dr. Norman Bethune graduated from the Faculty of Medicine in this building. It was demolished in 1967 and the site is now occupied by the Medical Sciences Building.

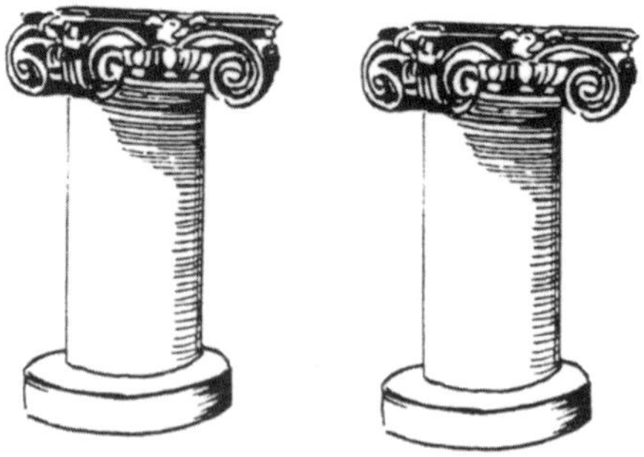

10. **Sherbourne Street Residences**
polished granite columns with red sandstone bases and capitals

The granite columns are from row housing on Sherbourne Street.

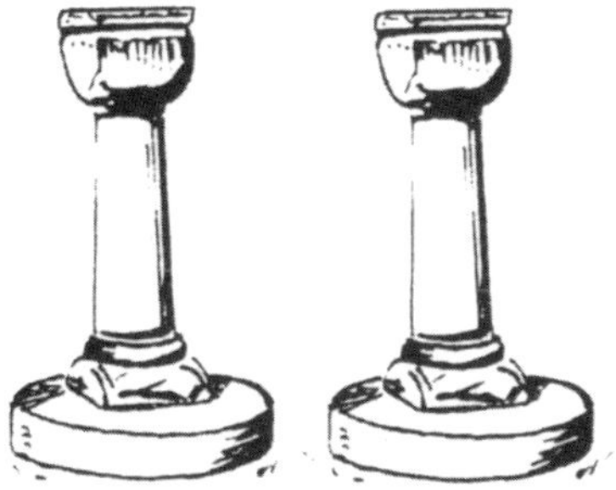

11. **University of Toronto window well** (one of two)

12. **Rosedale residence columns**
two limestone columns with Corinthian capitals

The limestone columns are from a large private residence in Rosedale. The house was demolished in 1948 for the extension of Mount Pleasant Road.

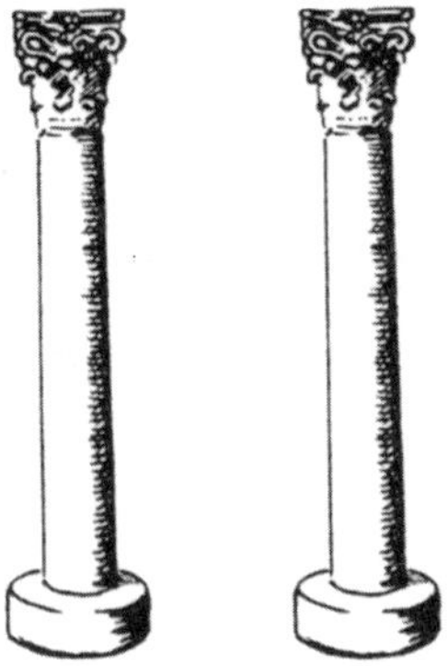

13. **Toronto Globe and Mail panel**
(On the wall of the Guild office)

The carved limestone panels once graced each side of the main entrance. The building was built in 1938 and demolished in 1974 when the site became part of First Canadian Place.

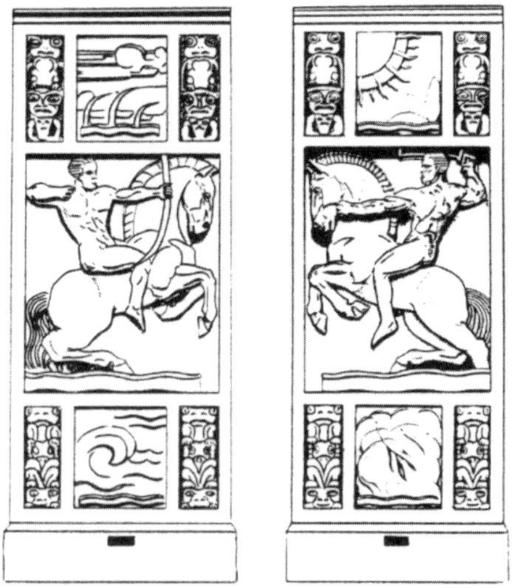

14. **Armories—Margurette stone**

North of Osgood Hall, on the east side of University Avenue, was the location of the Amouries building. The margurette was one of two built into the face of the building, built in 1891. The building was demolished in 1963, now the site of the Central Court House.

15. **Toronto Gobe and Mail panel**
(See previous page)

16. **The Guild Office Building**

Spencer Clark once had his office in this building.

Guild Inn Patio

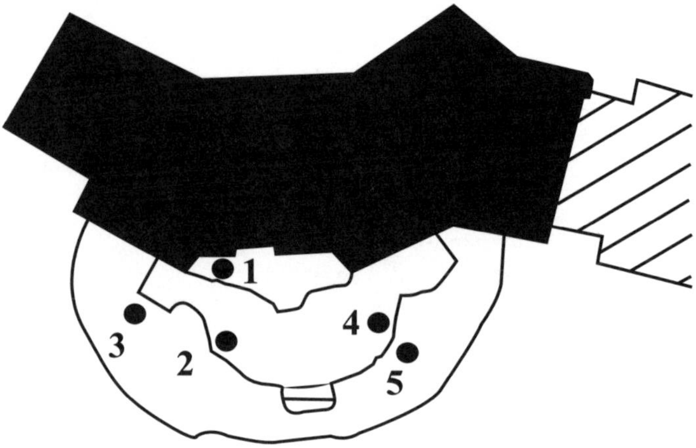

Guild Inn Patio

1. **Ballustrade fragment**

   There is no information on where this came from.

2. **Richmond Building Bas Relief Carvings**
   double sided

   one side—Ruebens
   second side—Columbus

3. **Imperial Oil Ltd. Cornerstone**

This building was originally the city of York's Court House (1824-1853) where the gaol, stocks and gallows were located. The Imperial Oil Limited head office at 92 King Street East, was part of the Court House Square. The building was demolished in 1969.

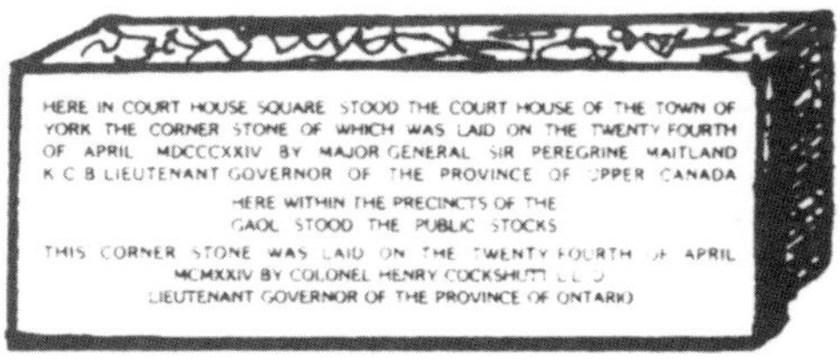

4. **Oxford University Press—Amen House**

This building was once located at 480 University Avenue. It was built in 1929 and demolished in 1964. In London, England, friars processed singing and sang AMEN at a certain corner. This corner became known as the Amen corner. Oxford Press built its first head office on this corner.

5. **Raphael**
bas-relief portrait from the Richmond Building

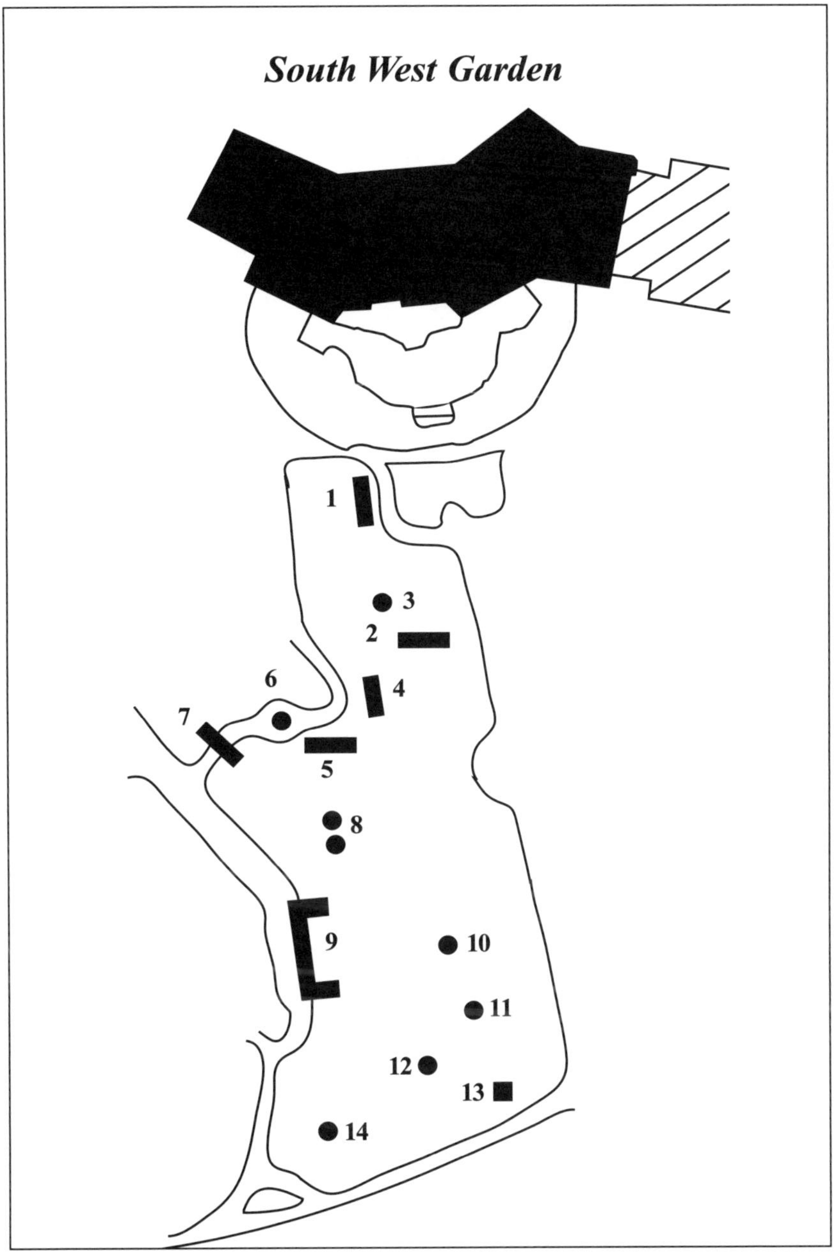
South West Garden
1
3
2
6
4
7
5
8
9
10
11
12
13
14

South West Garden

1. Imperial Bank of Canada Entrance

The entire marble facacade (the false front of a building) including the pediment (a low triangular gablelike decoration over a door or window), and fluted columns were preserved from the Imperial Bank of Canada building. The building was constructed in 1928 and demolished in 1972. This site now contains the 34 storey Canadian Imperial Bank of Commerce building at 2 Bloor Street West.

Beneath the marble facade is a female statue known as Musidora.

2. Grindstone

The Goldie family of Galt, Ontario, brought this grindstone to Canada from Ireland. The grindstone was made in 1860 and many Ontario plowshares and mower blades were sharpened on it.

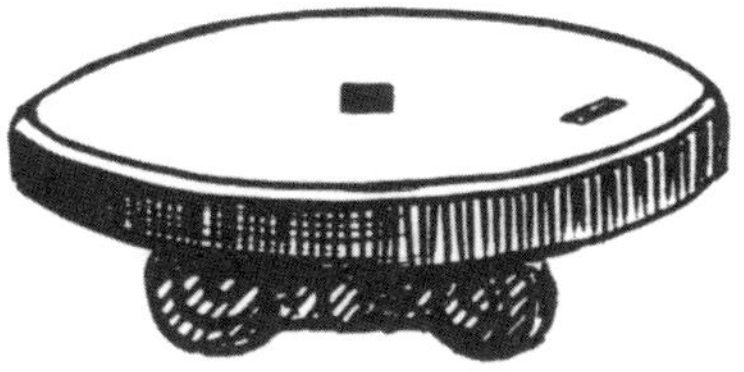

3. Bank of Nova Scotia—Exterior Entrance

The main entrance at 39 King Street West to the Bank of Nova Scotia, is made from Ohio sandstone and was built in 1903. The bank was there until 1951 when it built a new office across the street. A public library used this building then the Canadian Imperial Bank of Commerce. In 1969 the building was demolished.

Exterior Entrance—Ohio Sandstone

4. Bank of Nova Scotia stone carvings

Stone faces and decorative features from the Bank of Nova Scotia occupy one side of this wall. On the reverse side are pieces from the Quebec Bank. The Quebec Bank building was constructed in 1912 and demolished in 1969 for the Commerce Court. In 1917 the Quebec Bank merged with the Royal Bank.

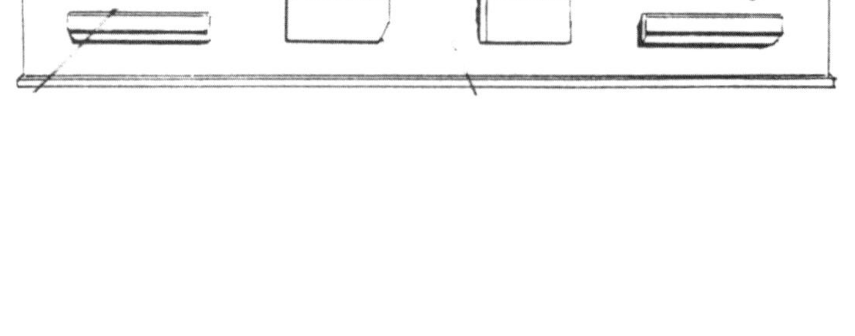

5. Provincial Paper Ltd.
And Abitibi Power and Paper Company Ltd.
Canadian Bank of Commerce

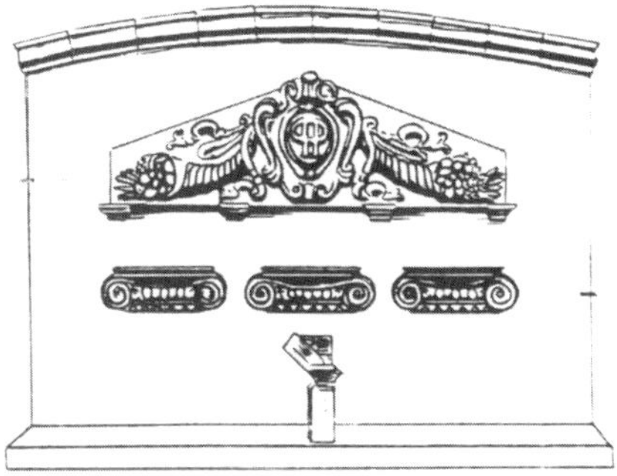

This wall contains pieces from three buildings. The top piece is from the Provincial Paper Building which stood at 394 University Avenue, beside the Abitibi Building. Three iconic capitals (top part of an architectural column) are in the centre of the wall. Below them are carved stone pieces from the Bank of Toronto. These two buildings were constructed in 1930 and demolished in 1968.

On the reverse side are art nouveau-style pieces of Ohio sandstone from the Canadian Bank of Commerce. In 1961 this bank merged with the Canadian Imperial Bank. The building was built in 1899, 796 Yonge Street, and demolished in 1972. Until 1854 this site was a burial ground for strangers and people who couldn't be buried in regular cemetaries.

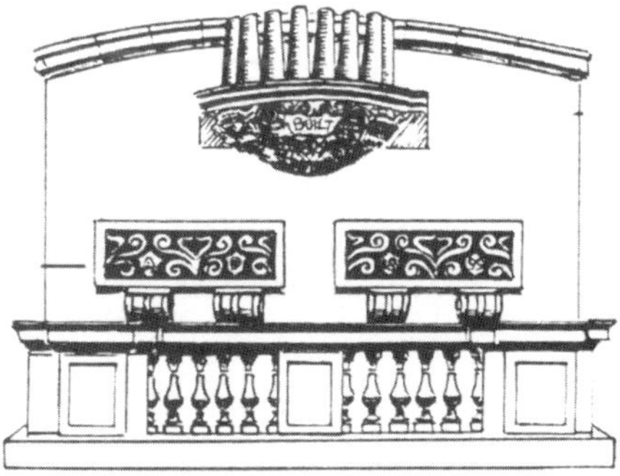

6. Registry of Deeds and Land Titles Column

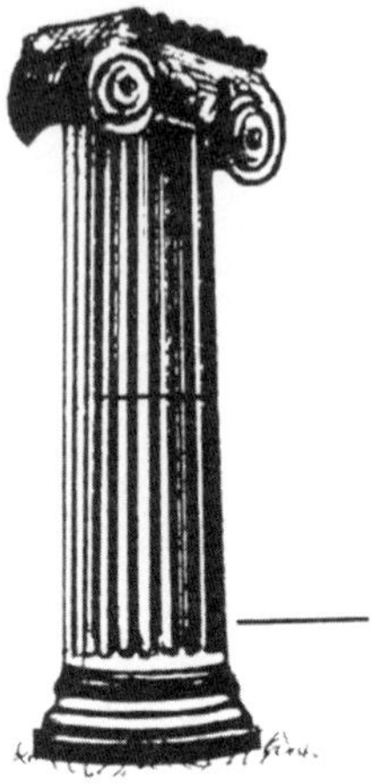

This fluted column and Ionic capital was preserved from the main entrance of the building, an example of Greek architecture. Built in 1915 the building was demolished in 1964, and the site now occupied by underground parking for the Toronto City Hall. It is half the height that it was before demolition.

7. R.H. King Collegiate Institute

Constructed of bricks and Indiana limestone, this structure was once a boy's entrance to the school. In 1976 this building was demolished to build a larger school, which remains on the original site at Kingston Road and St. Clair Avenue.

8. Bank of Toronto Columns

A Canadian marble quarry near Bancroft, Ontario, supplied the material to build these columns. Eight of the columns were used to build the Greek Theatre. The Bank of Toronto building was constructed in 1912. In 1955 this bank merged with the Dominion Bank, thus becoming the Toronto Dominion Bank. The building was demolished in 1966.

9. The Greek Theatre

(See the section on the Greek Theatre pg. 261)

10. **Solstice—Kosso Eloul**

Painted steel, this sculpture was made for the exhibit of Contemporary sculpture to celebrate the Inn's 50 years of operation (1982). Kosso was born in Russia in 1920.

11. **Mill Stone**

This segemented limestone mill stone is thought to have come from Galt, Ontario. There is another mill stone near the horse's head made of solid granite, possibly from Kingston, Ontario.

12. **Horse's Head—Sculptor Emanuel Hahn**

Draft horses played an important role in World War I. Emanuel created this sculpture to honour them. This bronze sculpture is on loan, courtesy of Emanuel's daughter Qennefer Browne.

13. **Block from Long Sault Canal**
near Cornwall, Ontario

Limestone blocks formed the sloping sides of the original St. Lawrence Seaway canal. Three blocks were salvaged before the old canal was submerged beneath fifty feet of water for a deeper canal.

14. **Bank of Montreal panels**

Manitoba	Elizabeth Wynn Wood
Saskatchewan	Elizabeth Wynn Wood
Alberta	Jacobine Jones
North West Territories	Emanuel Hahn

North-West Territories

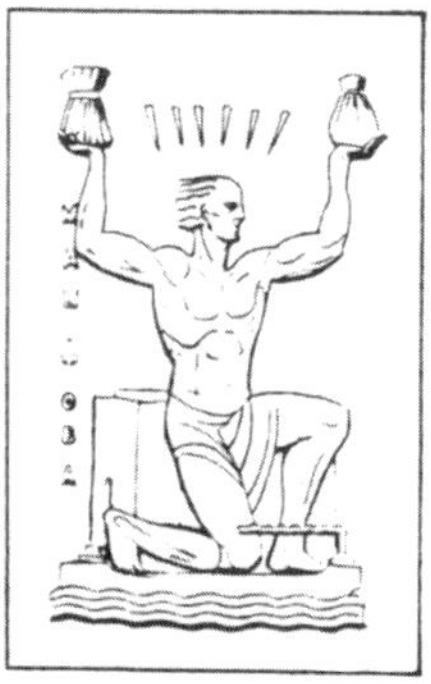

Manitoba

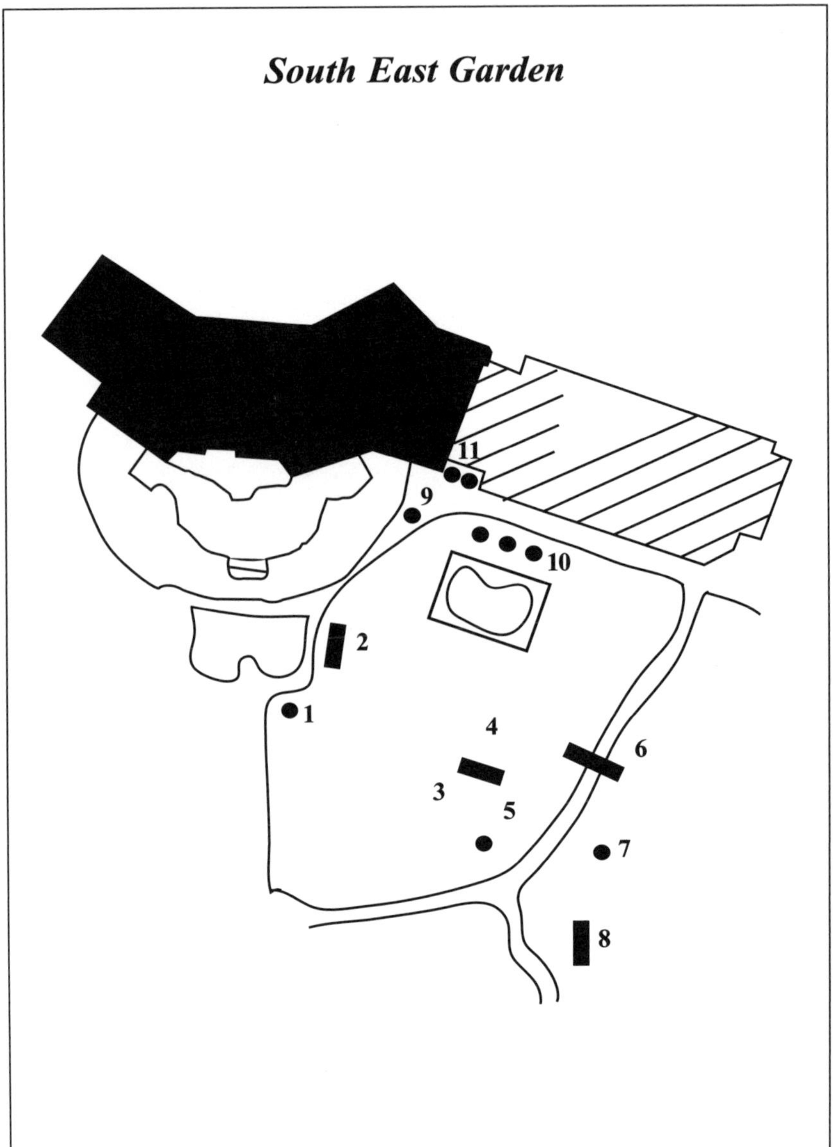
South East Garden
11
9
10
2
1
4
6
3
5
7
8

1. **Bank of Nova Scotia Columns**

These are more of the columns made from Ohio sandstone, of the Bank of Nova Scotia building demolished in 1969.

2. **Bank of Toronto Entrance**

This was one of the entrances into the Bank of Toronto at King and Bay Streets, constructed from Ontario marble.

3. Copper Panels—Frances Gage

4. Toronto Conservatory of Music

On the music wall are two copper bas-reliefs done by sculptor Frances Gage. The musicians depicted here are Dr. Healey Willan and Sir Ernest MacMillan.

Red sandstone was the material used to build the main entrance to the Toronto Conservatory of Music. Red terra-cotta was used for the entrance header. The building was constructed in 1897 and demolished in 1968. In 1936 the name was changed to the Royal Conservatory of Music.

5. **Bear (not a polar bear)**
Sculptors E.B. Cox and Michael Clay

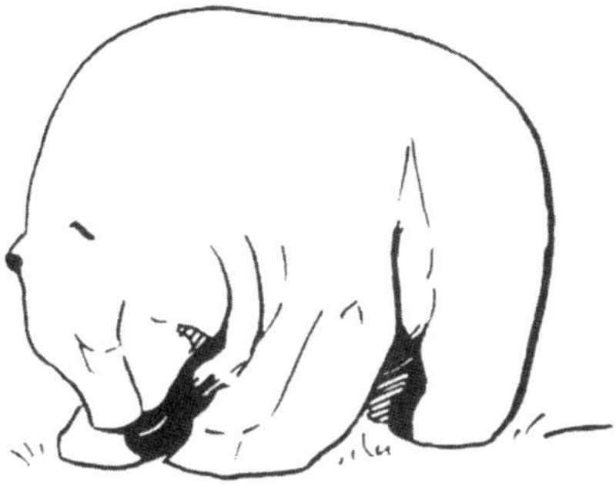

Because of its white colour, this bear has been erroneously labelled as a polar bear. However, the sculptor E.B. Cox states emphatically that this is a brown bear. A polar bear's nose is very different from the one carved here. The bear was sculpted on the grounds of the Inn in 1979 from portland limestone.

6. **The Granite Club Entrance**

This structure was the main entrance to the prestigious Granite Club on St. Clair Avenue. The stone carvings and fluted columns are made of Indiana limestone. In 1926 the building was completed and demolished in 1973. A condominium building now occupies this site. The Granite Club moved to a newer building on Bayview Avenue.

7. Robert Holmes Sculpture—Sculptor John Byers

Robert Holmes taught drawing for 30 years at Upper Canada College, and is noted for being the most famous painter, of his time, for drawing wild flowers. Made from granite, sculptor John Byers was inspired to do this work by Paul Breithaupt, Rosa Clark's younger brother.

8. **Toronto Star Building**

Architects in Toronto used the art deco style for a short period of time. These seven Indiana limestone blocks, and two ganite panels, were once part of the Toronto Star building built in 1929. Demolished in 1972, this site is now occupied by First Canadian Place.

9. **Chrysalides—Sculptor Antoine Poncet**

An outstanding sculptor, Antoine Poncet was born in Paris in 1928. He carved this sculpture from Labrador granite.

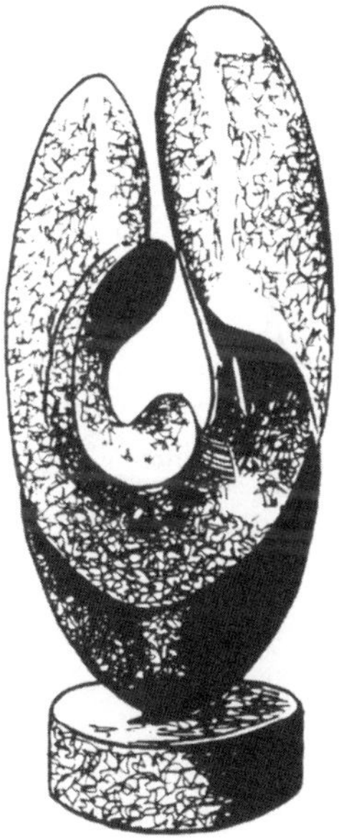

10. Bank of Toronto Panels

Attached to the wall of the upper terrace are three crest panels that were once above the entrance arches of the Bank of Toronto building at King and Bay Streets. One panel represents Enterprise. A second one represents Agriculture, and the third is the City of Toronto Coat of Arms.

Enterprise

Agricultrue

City of Toronto Coat of Arms

11. Bank of Montreal Panels

New Brunswick	Florence Wyle
Prince Edward Island	Florence Wyle
Newfoundland	Donald Stewart
The Artic	Emanuel Hahn

Rosa and Spencer Clark
beside the Bank of Toronto Panels
From the collection of The Guild

On the Bluffs

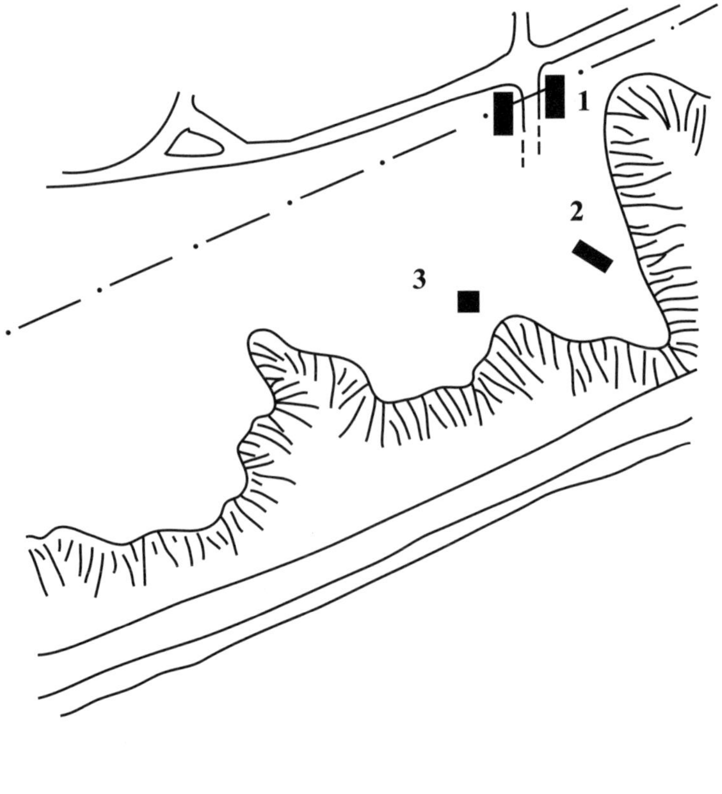

On the Bluffs

1. **Gateway to Scarborough Bluffs**

The wrought iron gates are from the Gibson House in the Rosedale area of Toronto, Ontario. The terra-cotta turets and octagonal piers (posts) are from the Produce Exchange Building which was built in 1890. In the 1950s the building was modernized and Spencer Clark acquired the piers and turets. The building was demolished in 1980.

2. **Block from Long Sault Canal**
   (See # 13—South West Garden)

3. **Tablet**

Wording: Scarborough Bluffs at the Guild Inn named in 1793 by Elizabeth Simcoe, wife of Lieutenant Govenor of Upper Canada after the world famous bluffs in Scarborough, England.

Demolished Sites

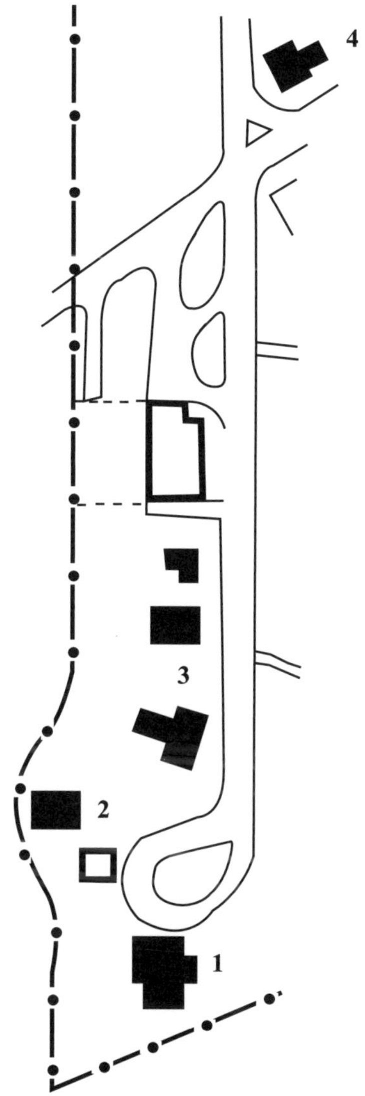

Demolished Sites

1. Corycliff
   (See section on Corycliff page 191)

2. Duncan Barn
   (See section on Duncan Barn page 231)

3. Three cottages

4. Cottage
   (See section on cottages page 215)

Sculptures Moved

1. **Fiesole—Sorel Etrog**
   - Removed by Sculptor

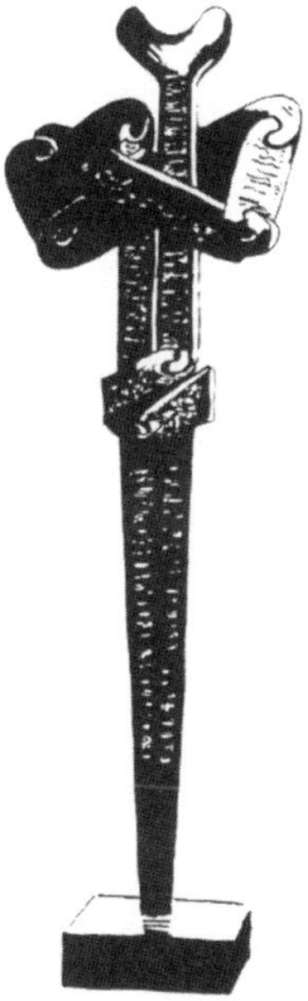

2. **Capriccio—Sorel Etrog**
   - Removed by Sculptor

3. **Source 1—Sorel Etrog**—Removed by Sculptor

4. **Two Acrobats—Sorel Etrog**—removed by sculptor after it was damaged by vandals.

5. **Swan Sculpture** from fountain—base cracked, repaired but no longer able to be outside. This sculpture was rescued from the Burlington Arcade in London, England, which was bombed in World War II. The sculptor was Peter Hills who did much of the restoration work on Westminster Abbey.

6. **St. Francis and the Wolf**—moved because someone tried to steal the statue. Hopefully it will someday be returned to the garden. (See the section on sculptor Thomas Bowie page 93)

7. **Moses and Aaron**—moved when the bases cracked. Originally they stood at the main entrance to the Inn and are pieces from the Canadian Northern Railway.

Aaron *Moses*

8. **Carved keystone**—Toronto General Post Office—was removed when the base cracked and are now in storage.

9. **Shell carving**—from The Ontario Bank—was used as a piece in the show Canada Blooms. Eventually it will be again be placed on its base, south of the bear.

KEYSTONE WALL—south west garden

This wall is composed of many pieces from various buildings. The benches are parts from the Imperial Oil Building.

Information

1904—The Breithaupt Family

Front row on footstool: William Walter
Second row L to R:
Louis Orville, Emma, Catherine, Paul, Louis Jacob, Edna
Back row standing:
Rosa, Lillian, Evelyn

Rosa Breithaupt Family Tree

Father—Louis Jacob Breithaupt
(m) Emma Alvarene Devitt—Mother

Louise Evelyn	1882–1939
Martha Edna	1885–1963
Rosa Melvina	1888–1981
William Walter	1894–1977
Louis Orville	1890–1960
Emma Lillian	1884–1951
Catherine Olive	1896–1977
Paul Theodore	1903–1962

Rosa Breithaupt (m) Russell Hewetson

Ruth 1920 . . . . married name Ruth Langley
Dorothy 1923 . . . . married name Dorothy Leonard
Rosemary(Posie) 1925 . . . . married name Posie Amell
Russell 1927

Rosa Breithaupt Hewetson (m) Spencer Clark

Rosa Breithaupt Hewetson Clark

Member of:

Life member of Royal Ontario Museum
Art Gallery of Ontario
Ontario Historical Society
Women's Canadian Historical Society
Robert Owen Foundation

Trustee of:

International Society of Christian Endeavour

Vice President of:

Women's Canadian Club

Awarded:

1978—Scarborough's Award of Merit

Honourary Pallbearers:

Prof. Eric R. Arthur
Hon. Margaret Birch
Col. James R. Breithaupt
Mr. Haskell Coates
Hon. Paul Cosgrove
Mr. George Cross
Hon. Wm. G. Davis
Mr. Sorel Etrog
Mr. Gordon M. Farquharson
Mr. Arthur Gelber
Mayor Augustus Harris
Col Robert H. Hilborn
Dr. Irwin Hilliard
Mr. Kenneth Jarvis
Mr. Henry E. Langford
Mr. Vincent Regan
Mr. Kenneth R. Thomson
Mr. Hugh Walker
Hon. Thomas Wells

Clark Family Tree

Father—John Ernest Clark
(m) Esther Louisa Alexander—Mother

John Alexander	1891–1950
Samuel Ernest	1894–1961
Florence Mabel	1896–
Herbert Spencer	1903–1986
Wilfred Harold	1905–

Spencer Clark

Member of:

University of Toronto—Alumni Association
—President's Committee
Life Member of Art Gallery of Ontario
Royal Ontario Museum
Ontario Historical Society
York Pioneers
Architectural Conservancy of Ontario
Metropolitan Toronto Board of Trade
Granite Club
Arts and Letters Club
Museum of Modern Art
Ontario Institute of Painters
Student Christian Movement
International Society of Christian Endeavour
Robert Owen Foundation

Honourary Member of:
Royal Architectural Institute of Canada
International Association of Architects

Awarded:

1978	Scarborough's Award of Merit
1983	Order of Canada
1984	Special Award—Toronto Historical Board
1985	Gold Medal
	Royal Canadian Academy of Arts Medal
	Doctor of Laws—University of Waterloo

Honourary Pallbearers:

Hon. John B. Aird
Mr. Wm. E. Bergey
Hon. Margaret Birch
Mr. Douglas C. Borden
Dr. A.J. Casson
Mr. Haskell Coates
Mr. Robert R. Cranston
Mr. George E. Cross
Hon. Wm. G. Davis
Mr. Sorel Etrog
Mr. Gordon M. Farquharson
Mr. Arthur E. Gelber
Mayor Augustus Harris
Dr. Irwin Hilliard
Mr. Kenneth Jarvis
Dr. Douglas H. Johnson
Mr. Gene Kinoshita
Mr. Charles A.G. Matthews
Hon. Pauline McGibbon
Rt. Hon. D. Roland Mitchener
Dr. Clark H. Pinnock
Mr. Ross Pinnock
Mr. F. Vincent Regan
Mr. Kenneth Thomson
Mr. J. Bryan Vaughan
Mr. Hugh P. Walker
Dr. Douglas Wright
Mr. Kenneth Yates

The Guild of All Arts

Batik
Keith Hartwell
Alice McCabe
C.J. Travers

Block Prints
J.H.W. Bradfield

Cabinet Making
W.J. Robidoux

Ceramics
Mr. Bardley

Enamel
Beth McLaughlin

Etchings, Aquatints, Engravings
Nicholas Hornyansky

Jewelery and Decorative Ware
Marjorie Stokes

Marquetry
Harvard Reddick

Musicians
Boris Berlin
Cecil Burnham-Kappey
Prof. Clark
McGill University
Margaret Empringham
Boris Hamburg
Clement Hamburg

Musicians (cont'd)
Mark Hamburg
Virginia Knott
Sir Ernest MacMillan
Reginald Stewart

Painting and Drawing
Gaile Thompson Campbell
W.H. Carswell
A.J. Casson
Rody Kenney Courtice
Dorothy Dick
Joachim Gauthier
Nicholas Hornyansky
E.L. Thompson
R. Wilcox

Pewter and Copper
Douglas Boyd
Keith Hartwell
Franz Kral
1937–1943
Harold Stacey

Photography
Orville Allen
"Jay" Jaycocks
Frank Pogue

Printing
Erick Aldwinckle
Florence McGillivary
E.L. Thompson

Raffia
Violet Armstrong
Jean Ford
Marjorie Lee

Sculpture
Thomas Bowie
1953–1964
John Byers
Gaile Thompson
Campbell
Michael Clay
1979–1996
E.B. Cox
Dorothy Dick
Sorel Etrog
Frances Gage
Dorsey James
1979–1990
Kenneth Jarvis
Aage Madsen
Frank Mildred
Siggy Puchta
E.L. Thompson
Arthur Tracy
Elizabeth F.
Williamson
1971–1995

Shell Pictures
Anne Kellet

Silver Work
Arthur Nevil Kirk
1935

Spinning
Alice McCabe

Stone Mason
Arthur Hibberd

Tooled Leather
Muriel Burnaby
Walter Goforth
Martha McCully

Weaving
W.C. Dawson
Margaret Hartwell
Kathleen Hunt
Alex MacDowell
Grace Pogue

Wood Carving
Thomas Bowie
Tom Feenstra
—1980–1983
Dorsey James
Aage Madson
Alfred Perry
Gerd Untermann
1980–1981

Woodworking
Frank Carrington
Frank Mildred
Clarence Nelson
Herman Riedl
N. Turner

Wrought Iron
A.E. Freeman
Jack Freeman
J. Wylie Freeman
Robert Freeman

Building Extensions

1934	A kitchen was built with offices above on the west side of the building.
1937	Section added to the front for a crafts room, an entrance lobby between the Coral Dining Room which is now called the York Wilson Room which was once the library.
1941–42	East wing added with conference rooms on the first floor and guest rooms on the second and third floor. This addition was called the Jackson wing for the man who partially financed the construction costs.
1947–48	Laundry facilities were built on the west side of the Inn with administration offices above after Scarborough Hall was closed by the government.
1955	Receiving entrance constructed on the west side of the building, at the back.
1958–63	Maintenance rooms built at the front of the Inn on west side of the building.
1965	East wing added, six floors, for guests and conferences, including an elevator.
1968	Lounge added to the original terrace and called the Heritage Lounge.

Special Visitors

Lorne Green—Actor from the TV show "Bonanaza"

Eric Christmas—Actor from musicals, Stratford Theatre

John Drainie—Actor from musicals, Stratford Theatre

Rex Loring—TV newscaster, announcer, interviewer

Max Ferguson—Actor, musician from Rawhide series, Old Country Music

Percy Saltzman—weatherman from CBC, lecturer

Bruce Marsh—News and sports commentator

Harry J. Boyle—TV producer

Arthur Hailey—Author, playwright

Cecilia Franca—Ballerina, world famous

Sir Cedric Hardwicke—Actor

Lillian and Dorothy Gish—Silent film actresses

Noira Shearer—Ballet dancer

Rex Harrison—Actor, musical comedy star

Lilly Palmer—Actress, former wife of Rex Harrison

Sir John Gielguid—Actor and director

Imogene Cocoa—Actress and comedy star

Anne Brown—Actress from Porgy & Bess

Glen Gould—Musician

George Gobel—Comedian, singer

Wallace Havelock Robb—Distinguished poet

Prime Minister Lester B. Pearson—Canada

Barbara Ann Scott—World famous figure skater

Sir Lawrence Olivier—Dramatic actor

Street Definitions

Avenue: . . . . .concession streets or border roads in a subdivision

Boulevard: . . . . . . .all collector roads in a subdivision

Court: . . . . .a cul de sac longer than 400'

Crescent: . . . . .a full or partial crescent—not more than 1000' in length

Drive: . . . . .streets of the same design but longer than a crescent

Gate: . . . . .a short street providing an entrance to a subdivision or to another street

Place: . . . . .a closed curve or cul de sac less than 400' long

Road: . . . . .all streets running north and south in a subdivision

Square: . . . . .a four sided shape forming a square usually in an open space surounding a park or a monument

Street: . . . . .all thoroughfares running in an east-west direction through a subdivision

Trail: . . . . .a winding street not too long that orginated as a nature trail or path through a wooded section

Terrace: . . . . .opposite a park or an open space where the terrain rises higher than street level

Walk: . . . . .pedestrians only

Street Names

Bethune . . . . .named after Dr. Norman Bethune, a doctor who went to China

Catalina . . . . .an island off the coast of California, USA

Earswick . . . . .the model town in Yorkshire, England of the Rowntree Chocolate company

Bledlow Manor . . . . .in England this was the home of Spencer Clark's grandmother

Bournville . . . . . .the model worker's town in England built by Cadbury's Chocolates

Sonneck Square . . .an old castle on the Rhine River in Germany

Sir Raymond . . . . .named after Sir Raymond who planned a model village in Manchester, England

Prince Philip . . . . .after Queen Elizabeth's husband

Nuffield Dr. . . . . . .after Lord Nuffield and his connection with Rowntree Chocolates

Rowatson . . . . .after Robert Watson McClain who owned the farm where the street is

Sonneck Circle . . .a name connected with Rosa Clark's family

Toynbee Trail . . . . .Rosa and Spencer had close connections with Toynbee Hall where MacKenzie King and other great men lived while studying in England

Cadbury Court . . . .after the pioneering work of the Cadbury family

Somerdale Square .honours the Frys for early comunity projects

Livingston Road . .at one time, 50 acres was called Livingston Park, named after the owner who was treasurer of the T. Eaton Company

Westlake Road . . . .was named after brothers who were involved in real estate and owned the property with another man, Cecil White, and were responsible for developing the area into 50' wide lots

Acknowledgements

Thank you to everyone who took the time to talk to me, gave me information and answered all my questions. Without you, this book could not have been written.

Avdichuk, Alexandra	The Guild
Beckman, Margaret	daughter of sculptor Thomas Bowie
Bellingham, Susan	Head of Special Collections, University of Waterloo
Bickford, Harold D.	information on his family
Boutilier, Alicia	information on Rody Kenny Courtice
Bowie, Alan	son of sculptor Thomas Bowie
Britton, Jane	University of Waterloo
Cranley, Father Bob	Archivist, Scarborough Foreign Mission
Daniel, Betty	daughter of woodworker Clarence Nelson who sent me her father's memoirs
Ellis, Anne	daughter of woodworker Herman Riedl
Gibson, Sally	Metro Archives
Hampson, Lindy	former employee of the Guild Inn
Hewetson, Russell	son of Rosa Hewetson Clark
Hurn, Nancy	Metro Archives
Langley, Ruth	daughter of Rosa Hewetson Clark
Leonard, Dorothy	daughter of Rosa Hewetson Clark
MacDonald, Nancy	former housekeeper of the Guild Inn
Pogue, David	information on his family and his personal memories
Purmal, Gregory	information on the Bickford family
Schofield, Richard	Chair of Scarborough LACAC
Seager, Dianne	University of Waterloo, Rare Books Room
Simpson, Florence	caregiver to Rosa Clark
Stepanian, Maggy	University of Toronto, Scarborough Campus, for the location of the cairn and plaque to Lucy Doyle
Walker, Hugh	former Curator of the Guild Inn
Yeoman, Philip	information on Walter Goforth

Index

Bibliography

Books

4 Women Who Painted in the 1930s and 1940s, Alicia Boutilier
A.J. Casson—An Artist's Life, Christopher Jackson
Contemporary Outdoor Sculpture at the Guild, 1982
Dictionary of Canadian Artists, Colin S. MacDonald
Art Gallery of Northumberland, Gage, 1997
Hands on Rigid Heddle Weaving, Betty Linn Davenport
Library of the World's Myths and Legends—Scandinavian Mythology, H.R. Ellis Davidson—1982
Siggy Puchta—Sculptor, Self-published 1978
Sunnybrook Health Science Centre—1948–1993
The Complete Handbook of Leather Crafting, Jane E. Garner
The Technique of Weaving, John Toney
The Spencer Clark Collection of Historic Architecture, Hugh Walker
The Girls, Rebecca Sisler
The Merriam, Webster Dictionary, New Edition, 1994

Magazines

Toronto Life, Vol 31–No. 13, September 1997—page 106

From the files of:

Metro Toronto Archives
The Guild
Breithaupt Hewetson Clark Collection, University of Waterloo
Memories of David Pogue
Memoir of Clarence Nelson

Newspaper articles from the files of The Guild:

The Toronto Daily Star
The Evening Telegram
The Scarborough Mirror
The News/Post
Toronto Globe & Mail

About the Author—Carole M. Lidgold

An imaginative child, Carole was always writing stories and poetry that she never let anyone see. In her adult years she joined the Canadian Authors Association as well as enrolling in nightschool writing courses. Letters to the editor brought notority and she unsuccessfully attempted politics. Articles she wrote were published in magazines and newspapers, and she began self-publishing books.

Carole is married to Gordon, with one daughter Lorraine, two grandchildren Alex and Lindsay. Her pets include Sheba and Lucky, two dogs, and an old cat, Mr. Tommie Blue Socks.

Other Books by Carole M. Lidgold

Adult:
Journey Into Christmas
Faces of the Night

Children:
The Adventures of Inch Worm Willie
The Elf Who Made Snowflakes
Daisy Dee's Party

Historical:
Memories of Cayuga—Ontario's Love Boat
Steamship Cayuga—Toronto's Ship of Romance

Stage Play:
Counsellor on Marriage—*A comedy*

Published by Questex Consulting Ltd., 1999.
Brookridge Publishing House
Box 11041, 97 Guildwood Parkway
Scarborough, Ontario M1E 5G5